# aristotle and the elements

Aristotle believed that the "simple bodies" of fire, air, water, and earth were each made from two of the "elements" of hot, cold, moist, and dry. He also thought that the simple bodies could change into each other by exchanging one of their component elements—fire (dry and hot) could change into air (moist and hot) by exchanging the dry for moist. Similarly, air could exchange its hot for cold to become water. He depicted this theory of behavior as a pattern of change, where each simple body could change into another until the process came full circle.

# Inspired Fair Isle Knits

## 20 Creative Designs Inspired by the Elements

### FIONA ELLIS

POTTER
CRAFT

New York

All rights reserved.
Published in the United States by
Potter Craft, an imprint of the Crown Publishing Group,
a division of Random House, Inc., New York.
www.crownpublishing.com
www.pottercraft.com

POTTER CRAFT and colophon, and POTTER and
colophon are registered trademarks of Random House, Inc.
Library of Congress Cataloging-in-Publication Data

Ellis, Fiona.
Inspired Fair Isle knits : 20 creative designs
inspired by the elements / by Fiona Ellis. — 1st ed.
p. cm.
Includes index.
ISBN-13: 978-0-307-34686-5 (hardcover : alk. paper)  1.  Knitting—Patterns.
2.  Sweaters. 3.  Knitting—Scotland—Fair Isle—Patterns.  I. Title.

TT825.E454 2007
746.43'2041—dc22
2007007601
ISBN:  978-0-307-34686-5
Printed in China

Cover and graphic design by Caitlyn Daniels Israel
Photography by Lindsay Maier
Photographs on pages 26 and 100 © Kristin Sorton
Photograph on page 74 courtesy iStockphoto ™ (www.istockphoto.com)
Photograph on page 50 courtesy Paul Edmondson/Photodisc/Getty Images

Illustrations by Rebecca Cober

1 3 5 7 9 10 8 6 4 2

First Edition

# dedication

To my Gran who taught me how to knit, and many other skills,
but encouraged me to use my imagination above all other things.

# contents

# water

## air

# fire

# earth

# introduction

KNITTING IS A TRADITIONAL CRAFT, linked both to the past and to the future by the thread of current practice. Even though many of the techniques we use in knitting have been around for practically forever, there are always new ways of using them to achieve fashionable and contemporary-looking garments.

I trained as a fashion designer and have always been an avid hand-knitter. I find that I approach my work by attempting to meld the traditional with the modern—this juxtaposition is a constant source of fascination to me. As I am designing, one part of my mind is thinking about the overall look of the garment and how it will fit into today's wardrobe choices. Another part of my mind is considering how I can give knitters a new way of approaching and working with traditional knitting methods.

The inspiration and concept for *Inspired Fair Isle Knits* evolved from my love of nature. I allowed each of the four elements—as defined in Western culture—to influence my selection of color palette, yarn, Fair Isle patterning, garment styling, trim details, and inclusion of additional stitches or techniques in each chapter. Look for the sidebars throughout the book; they all relate to the element that inspired the chapter and will stimulate the mind along with the needles.

In the pages to follow, you will learn to challenge the traditions of Fair Isle knitting. You will work with and challenge each of the following notions:

- **Placement of the patterning on the garment** Rather than having the patterning cover the whole garment, as in many traditional sweaters, I selected specific unconventional areas for placing the Fair Isle, such as at the cuff and shoulder (Whisper, page 70) or on the lower half of a raglan sleeve (Nautical, page 26).

- **Color placement or striping within the patterning** Color change is one of the most fun parts of knitting Fair Isle. It is also fun to design these changes—especially if they are not symmetrical or expected (Drifting, page 58; Sunkissed, page 76; Hearth, page 80) or repeated in simple stripes in another part of the garment (Toasty, page 94).

- **Mood that the patterning evokes** Patterning can create a feeling or mood that doesn't need to be predictable; it can give an illusion of swirling movements (Sway, page 52; Swirl, page 66) or be very graphic-looking (Hearth, page 80; Glowing, page 84).

- **Symmetry and repetition of patterning** Conventional Fair Isle patterns are repeated continuously across a row and are symmetrical both vertically and horizontally. I have given you repeats that change across the row (Crystal, page 38; Petroglyph, page 114), and nonsymmetrical, organic-looking patterning (Drifting, page 58; Peat, page 102; Glen, page 108; Kindle, page 88).

- **Stitchwork and technique combinations** Combining stitch techniques, methods, and different patterns can add lots of interest when working on a project and prevent us from getting bored. Many projects in this collection have combined Fair Isle with other techniques such as cables (Waves, page 30), lace patterning (Swirl, page 66; Whisper, page 70), felting (Canyon, page 120; Glen, page 108), or even pleats (Sway, page 52).

- **Types of garments** When we think of traditional Fair Isle garments, practical sweaters to be worn outdoors come to mind. But the technique can also be used for garments with completely different end uses. There are many sweaters included in this collection, but there are some surprises, too: a halter top (Sunkissed, page 76), a tank (Spindrift, page 34), and a wrap (Swirl, page 66).

The projects may sound as though they are aimed only at experienced knitters. Indeed, many of the projects are designed to challenge accomplished knitters, but many others will appeal to knitters new to the Fair Isle technique. In those projects, either the patterning is interspersed with areas of stockinette or, because you will felt the color work after knitting, any imperfections will be hidden.

# things you need to know before you begin

## What Is Fair Isle Knitting?

Fair Isle knitting is a traditional knitting technique that originally used small geometric motifs repeated across a row. The overall appearance can give the impression that, because many colors have been used, it is a complicated form of patterning. In fact, the technique used in this book never uses more than two colors in any one row. The term *Fair Isle* is now used to describe any knitting pattern that uses two different colors of yarn in the same row. The color not being used is carried across the back of the work and picked up later. It produces a warm fabric because of the extra layer created on the wrong side. Fair Isle patterns are worked in stockinette to show off the color patterns.

WORKING WITH TWO COLORS: STRANDING AND WEAVING IN Both the stranding and weaving methods may be used together within one row; the method used depends entirely on how many stitches the yarn needs to be carried over.

STRANDING If the pattern requires a color to be carried over fewer than five stitches, the stranding method is used. The second color is left at the back of the work

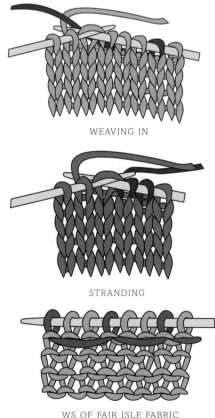

WEAVING IN

STRANDING

WS OF FAIR ISLE FABRIC

until it is needed. When it is next required, the second color is simply picked up, and work continues using it, leaving the first color at the back of the work until it is next needed. The stranded yarn floats on the wrong side of the fabric.

It is important to loosely carry the yarn that's not in use on the wrong side of the piece, but not too loosely. If the yarn being stranded is pulled too tightly, the result will be puckered or uneven fabric on the right side. To avoid this mistake, slightly stretch out the stitches on the right-hand needle that have just been worked before picking up the stranded yarn again.

WEAVING IN When a second color is to be carried over more than five stitches, it needs to be secured by the working yarn on every third stitch. This is called the *weaving method*. The weaving method maintains the elasticity of the fabric and avoids creating long floats, which increase the chance of puckering. To secure the second color, simply lay it over the working yarn or loop it over or under the working yarn before working the next stitch.

The weaving method can also be used when carrying one color up the side of the piece for just a few rows; simply twist the first color around the second color every two rows.

It is possible to weave in the second color after every stitch but doing so produces a very dense fabric. The projects in this book did not employ the weaving method after each stitch.

## Sizes

When selecting the size you wish to make, please refer to the schematic diagrams for your chosen project. The diagrams give the dimensions each pattern will produce when knitted at the gauge for that project. I suggest that you measure a garment that you already have and like the fit of; then choose the size that is closest to it based on the schematic diagram.

## Gauge

This is very important! Before you begin, please check your gauge carefully by knitting a swatch. Doing so will ensure that you achieve a desirable fabric and the correct size garment. To make a swatch, cast on enough stitches to be able to work at least a full repeat of the

pattern indicated; this may mean that you will be working a swatch larger than 4" [10cm]. Once you have made and blocked your swatch, measure it in several places to confirm its measurements. If you have more stitches and rows than the instructions indicate, rework the swatch using larger needles. If you have fewer stitches and rows, rework the swatch using smaller needles. See the section below for tips on working a gauge swatch in the round.

## Working in the Round

Some of the pattern instructions included in this book are given for working the project *in the round*. This means that you will use a circular needle and work round and round, rather than back and forth in rows as you do when making a flat garment piece. When working in this way, knitting every round produces stockinette fabric.

To keep track of the rounds, you will need to place markers to indicate the beginnings of the rounds. Take great care when joining the first round; it is very easy to twist the stitches, and once you have done that, it is impossible to untwist them. To avoid twisting them as you join the first round, take the time to ensure that all the stitches are aligned with the bottom edge or the underside of the needle and that no stitches are forming a spiral around the needle.

### WORKING GAUGE IN THE ROUND

You may find that while working in the round, your gauge will differ from working stockinette back and forth (knit one row, purl one row). When you work

stockinette stich in the round you are not working any purl rows. So I strongly suggest that, if you are working in the round, you should work a gauge swatch in the round also. This means that you will need to cast on more stitches than the number indicated to produce 4" [10cm].

## Charts and How to Read Them

Charts are visual representations of the knitted fabric (viewed from the right side) in diagram form. Each square represents one stitch, and a line of squares represents one row.

Begin at the bottom and work toward the top when following the charts, just as you knit. When working flat garment pieces, read from right to left for right-side rows and from left to right for wrong-side rows. When working in the round, read every round from right to left. To help you remember to switch the orientation, the row number appears at the side where you will begin. A ruler or piece of card to slide along the diagram as you work will help in reading row by row.

Fair Isle charts in this book are worked to produce stockinette fabric unless otherwise indicated.

## Pattern Repeats and Placing Markers

Pattern repeats are indicated by solid lines on the charts and by an asterisk (*) in the written instructions. The number of stitches in a repeat is shown at the base of each chart. Use this number as a guide when placing markers to indicate placements of different patterns across a row.

Using markers reduces the amount of stitch-counting necessary and aids in troubleshooting if you make a mistake. Some instructions will indicate precise placement of markers for clarity—when shaping is occurring, for example. You may also choose to use them in cases where they're not specifically called for.

Row counts for each repeat are shown at the bottoms of the charts.

## Sleeve Increases

Particularly when working sleeves, read through all instructions before you begin. Sometimes the instructions will give patterning details that need to be worked *at the same time* as increases.

## Finishing

I highly recommend blocking all pieces before you begin to join each project. Blocking makes it much easier to join the seams, and it can even out any minor stitch imperfections. To block, lay out each piece on a flat padded surface and pin out the fabric to the dimensions given in the schematic diagram. Then place a damp cloth over the piece and either leave it until it's completely dry, or hold an iron just above the cloth, raising and lowering the iron, letting steam penetrate the fabric. To avoid crushing the fabric, do not press down on the piece. Leave the piece pinned out until it's completely cool and dry. Consult the yarn label for care information; yarns containing synthetic fibers should not be ironed.

There are many methods for joining seams, so I suggest consulting your knitting reference book when selecting a technique to use. In most instances in this book, you can use a mattress stitch unless a specific alternative method is indicated.

## Setting In Sleeves

Fold the sleeve in half and place a marker to indicate the center point at the top of the sleeve cap. Pin the sleeve into the armhole, matching your marker to the shoulder seam. Match any bound-off stitches at the beginning of the cap shaping to the bound-off stitches at the beginning of the armhole shaping on the body pieces. Then ease the remaining fabric into the armhole between these points and pin it in place. Stitch the fabric in place; then remove the pins.

## Weaving In Ends

Thread the end that is to be woven into a large-eyed blunt needle. Weave the needle in and out through the piece on the wrong side for approximately 2" [5cm]. Pull up the thread; then turn and weave it in and out in the opposite direction for a few stitches. Pull up the thread and cut off the end close to your work. Never weave in more than one end at a time, as doing so will produce an unsightly ridge on the right side of the fabric. Using a fine-gauge latch hook tool can save time; weave the hook end of the tool through the fabric on the wrong side for 2" [5cm], working toward the end to be woven in. Place the end in the hook, and pull back through the fabric to close the latch and "weave" the end in. Repeat while working in the opposite direction. Cut off the end close to your work.

# techniques

The following explanations are for the methods and techniques used in the pattern instructions.

BACK STITCH Beginning approximately ¼" [5 mm] from lower/upper edge, take the needle down through the work to the wrong side of the work at the lower/upper edge. *Bring the needle back through to the right side approximately ¼" [5mm] ahead of the original starting point. Pull up the thread. Take the needle back through to the wrong side again at the starting point for the previous stitch. Repeat from * to the end.

BUTTONHOLE STITCH This is also known as *blanket stitch,* but here the stitches are worked closely together and used for covering the rings in the Spindrift project (page 34). Hold the end of the yarn and the ring to secure them while working the first few stitches. Bring the sewing needle from the outside of the ring through the hole in the ring and the loop formed by the yarn. Pull up on the needle to tighten the yarn around the ring. Continue around until the ring is covered, working over the end of the yarn to secure. End by stitching into the first stitch.

CABLES When you're knitting cables, groups of stitches are worked in a different order from how they present themselves on the left-hand needle. For this method, a short double-pointed needle called a *cable needle* is used.

   Slip stitches from the left-hand needle onto the cable needle, and hold the stitches either at the back or front of the work (depending on the pattern being worked). Then work a second group of stitches from the left-hand needle. Finally, work the stitches held on the cable needle.

CROCHET CHAIN Make a loop on the hook using a slipknot. *Wrap the yarn over the hook, draw the yarn through the loop to make a new loop on the hook. Repeat from * to desired length.

DUPLICATE STITCH The duplicate stitch, as its name implies, is an embroidered stitch that is worked over the top of a knitted stitch, duplicating the path that the yarn took to form the knitted stitch.

   First, identify the bottom of the stitch to be dupli-cated (it will look like a V). Bring the sewing needle from the wrong side to the right side at the bottom of

stitch, then take it up to the right-hand side of the stitch above and slide the needle below this stitch from right to left, bringing it out on the left-hand side of the stitch. Next, bring the needle back down and through to the wrong side at the same point as the starting point.

FELTING Place the piece to be felted in a small laundry bag and toss it in the washing machine with a few larger items. (I suggest two or three pairs of jeans.) Wash on hot, with a cold rinse cycle using mild laundry soap. Pull the piece into shape and leave it to dry. *Note: It is more correct to call this technique fulling, which means* felting *a finished piece of knitting. The term felting refers to the method used to felt loose fibers together.*

I-CORD I-cords are made using a pair of double-pointed needles. Cast on the required number of stitches, and knit them. *Do not turn the needle. Simply slide the stitches to the opposite end of needle, pull the yarn across the back of the stitches and knit them once more. Repeat from * until you've attained the desired length.

A strand will be produced on the wrong side, but as you work, you will see that each end of the rows will curl toward the other to form a tube and enclose this strand.

MATTRESS STITCH With right sides facing, place the two pieces to be joined side by side. Bring the sewing needle from the wrong side to the right side on the first piece one stitch from the edge. *Pick up the strand between the first and second stitches on the second piece. Pick up the strand between the first and second stiches on the first piece. Pull up the yarn. Repeat from * along the seam. The yarn will form a figure eight shape (without the crossover) as you work.

RUNNING STITCH Making stitches approximately ¼" [5mm] long on both sides of the work throughout, bring the needle from the back to the front. *Take the needle through the work to the wrong side of work and then back through to the right side of work again, Pull up thread. Rep from * to end.

SETTING IN A ZIPPER Working on a flat surface (not on your knee) lay the zipper behind the opening with the zipper teeth along the edges. Pin the zipper in place; then, using a contrasting sewing thread and taking great care not to stretch or pucker the fabric, baste the zipper in place using a *running stitch*. Remove the pins. Now, using matching sewing thread, whipstitch the zipper tape to the wrong side of each front. Then, working on right side approximately 1 stitch away from the edge, stitch the zipper in place using matching sewing thread and backstitch. Remove the basting.

SHORT ROWS Short row shaping is used for shoulder shaping rather than the usual binding-off stitches. As you work across the row, the instructions will tell you to work a number of stitches. Wrap the next stitch, which prevents a hole from forming. Then turn the

work, leaving the remaining stitches unworked— referred to as held stitches.

- **Wrapping a Stitch** Work to a turn point. With the yarn in back, slip the next stitch purlwise to the right-hand needle. Bring the yarn to the front; then slip the same stitch back onto the left-hand needle. Turn your work and bring the yarn into position for the next stitch, wrapping the stitch as you do. When you work across all the stitches once again, pick up the wraps to prevent them showing on the right side of the fabric.

- **Picking Up Wraps** Work to a stitch that is wrapped. Insert the tip of the right-hand needle from the front under the wrap from the bottom up, then into the wrapped stitch as usual. Knit them together, making sure the new stitch comes out under the wrap.

SINGLE CROCHET Make a loop on the hook using a slipknot. *Insert the hook into the fabric from right side to wrong side. Pull up a second loop, drawing it through the fabric. Catch the yarn with the hook and draw it through both loops on the hook. One loop is now remaining on the hook. Repeat from *.

**3-NEEDLE BIND-OFF** This technique is used for joining seams by knitting them together rather than sewing them. It can be used decoratively, worked on the right side of the garment, using a contrast color.

Begin by having each set of stitches to be joined on separate needles. Place the garment pieces together as indicated in the instructions. Right sides together will produce a seam on the inside of the garment; wrong sides together will produce a seam visible on the outside of the garment. Both needles need to be pointing in the same direction at this point.

Using a third needle, knit the first stitch from one needle together with the first stitch from the second needle, *knit the next stitch from each needle together, bind off the first stitch on the right needle in the usual manner. Repeat from * to the end.

**WHIPSTITCH** Bring needle from the back to the front. *Take needle across at a right angle, approximately ¼" [5mm] away and through to the back. Then bring needle through to the front once more directly above end point of last stitch. Pull up thread. Repeat from * to end.

## needle sizes

| METRIC | U.S. SIZES | CANADIAN/ U.K. SIZES |
|--------|------------|----------------------|
| 10 | 15 | 000 |
| 9 | 13 | 00 |
| 8 | 11 | 0 |
| 7.5 | — | 1 |
| 7 | — | 2 |
| 6.5 | 10.5 | 3 |
| 6 | 10 | 4 |
| 5.5 | 9 | 5 |
| 5 | 8 | 6 |
| 4.5 | 7 | 7 |
| 4 | 6 | 8 |
| 3.75 | 5 | 9 |
| 3.5 | 4 | — |
| 3.25 | 3 | 10 |
| 3 | — | 11 |
| 2.75 | 2 | 12 |
| 2.25 | 1 | 13 |
| 2 | 0 | 14 |
| 1.75 | — | 15 |

# abbreviations

ALT alternate

APPROX approximate(ly)

BEG beginning

BO bind off

C cable

CB center back

CF center front

CM centimeters

CN cable needle

COLOR A, B, ETC. indicates contrast colors

CONT continue(ing)

DEC decrease(ing)

DPN(S) double-pointed needle(s)

END end(ing)

FOLL following

INC increase

INC2 increase 2 stitches by working knit 1, purl 1, knit 1 all into next stitch

K knit

K2TOG knit 2 stitches together

K2TOGB knit 2 stitches together through back of loops

LH left hand (as in "left-hand needle")

LHS left-hand side

M1 make 1 stitch by picking up the strand between the next 2 stitches

M/C main color

P purl

P2TOG purl 2 sts together

P2TOGB purl 2 stitches together through back of loop

P3TOG purl 3 stitches together

PATT(S) pattern(s)

PSSO pass the slipped stitch over

REM remaining

REP repeat

REV ST ST reverse stockinette stitch—purl on right-side rows, knit on wrong-side rows

RH right hand (as in "right-hand needle")

RHS right-hand side

RND(S) round(s)

RS right side

SL slip

SL1-K2TOG-PSSO slip 1 stitch, knit 2 stitches together, then pass the slipped stitch over the stitch made by the knit 2 together

SSK slip the next 2 stitches, one at a time, knitwise onto the right needle; then knit them together in that position using the left needle and working through front of the loops

ST(S) stitch(es)

ST ST stockinette stitch—knit on right-side rows, purl on wrong-side rows

TBL through back of loop

TOG together

WS wrong side

YB yarn back

YFON bring yarn forward and over needle

YFWD yarn forward

YO yarn over

YRN yarn

* designates the starting point for a repetition of a series of instructions

( ) alternative measurements or instructions

[ ] metric conversion

# glossary

**GARTER STITCH** Knit all rows.

**GARTER RIDGE** Two or more knit rows following stockinette or reverse stockinette.

**REVERSE STOCKINETTE STITCH** Purl right-side rows; knit wrong-side rows (reverse of stockinette).

**SEED STITCH** When worked over an odd number of stitches, Row 1: (knit 1, purl 1) to the last stitch, knit 1.

Row 2: repeat Row 1. When worked over an even number of stitches, Row 1: (knit 1, purl 1) to the end. Row 2: (purl 1, knit 1) to the end.

**STOCKINETTE STITCH** Knit on right-side rows; purl on wrong-side rows.

**WORK EVEN** Continue working without increasing or decreasing stitches.

# water

THE SOFT PITTER-PATTER OF SPRING RAIN, the torrential downpour of a summer storm, the shimmer of snowflakes, the crash of waves at the shore, or the rhythmic drip of raindrops from a leaf. We both fear and respect this element's power while enjoying its rejuvenating properties.

To interpret this element into projects, I chose a palette of blues, greens, and purples to evoke memories of deep, dark oceans, the sound of crashing waves, or the twinkle of snowflakes against a midnight sky. The yarns selected are smooth or shiny to recall water's reflective properties. The transparency of this element is mirrored in the openwork included in two of the projects. Incorporating wavy edges or textured patterns along with Fair Isle patterns that are reminiscent of waves or snowflakes further connects us to the movement we associate with water. The styling is loose and easy, producing garments that are comfortable to wear at the water's edge or on the slopes.

# nautical

## WOMEN'S RAGLAN SWEATER

The heat of summer often causes us to seek out the cooling effect of water—we find ourselves drawn to the seashore, a river, or a lake. So it is no surprise that our clothing for this season often suggests a nautical feeling.

Traditional Fair Isle patterning evokes the mood of a soft misty island landscape through the use of subtle changes in color. So to conjure up a feeling of bright sunlight over shimmering water, a palette of sharper contrasts was selected. Graphic patterns and wavy lines are used instead of the more traditional organic inspired patterns, and highlights of threaded cords are used to reference the ropes found in nautical settings.

### Sizes/Finished Chest Measurements

XS 35" [89 cm]

S 39" [99cm]

M 41" [104cm]

L 44" [112cm]

XL 47" [119cm]

2X 50" [127cm]

Instructions are given for the smallest size. If changes are necessary for larger sizes, the instructions are given in ( ). Where there is only one set of figures, this applies to all sizes.

### Materials

Young Touch Cotton DK by Estelle Designs (100% mercerized cotton; 114yds [105m]/ 50g ball)

M/C, shade 029: 13 (14-16-18-19-21) balls

Color A, shade 028: 2 (2-2-3-3-3) balls

Color B, shade 0310: 1 (1-2-2-2-2) balls

Color C, shade 0047: 1 (1-1-2-2-2) balls

Color D, shade 7565: 1 (1-1-2-2-2) balls

Pair of size 6 [4mm] needles, size 6 [4mm] circular needle (16" [40.5cm] long) for neckline, 4 stitch holders, size G/6 [4mm] crochet hook

Yarn amounts given are based on average requirements and are approximate.

### Gauge

24 sts and 28 rows = 4" [10cm] over St st on size 6 [4mm] needles

Take the time to check your gauge; change the needle size if necessary to obtain the correct gauge and garment size.

REFER TO TECHNIQUES ON PAGE 18 FOR: **Crochet Chain**

REFER TO GLOSSARY ON PAGE 23 FOR: **Seed Stitch**

### Notes on Decreases

When shaping raglans, work decs 1 st in from edges as follows:

RS rows, work dec at beg of row as ssk, work dec at end of row as k2tog.

WS rows, work dec at beg of row as p2tog, work dec at end of row as p2togb.

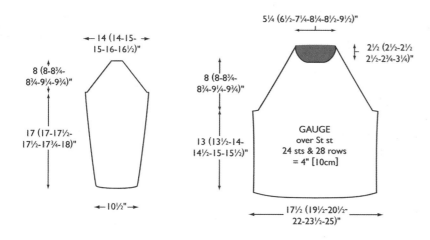

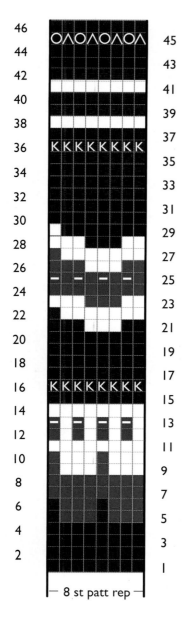

— 8 st patt rep —

Note: at end of row 45 work last YO as a k1.

## Key

- ■ M/C
- ◉ yo using M/C
- ◤ k2tog using M/C
- ■ Color A
- ◰ Knit using Color A (WS row)
- □ Color B
- ■ Color C
- ⊟ Purl using Color C (RS row)
- ■ Color D

Chart reads from R to L on RS rows, and from L to R on WS rows.

SHAPE FRONT NECK AS FOLLOWS

RS row: K1, ssk, k17 (23-23-26-31-33), turn (this is neck edge). Leave rem 34 (42-42-47-52-56) sts on a spare needle.

Working on the 19 (25-25-28-33-35) sts only, BO 4 sts at beg of next row, purl to end.

RS row: Dec 1 st at beg of row as before, knit to end.

WS row: BO 3 (3-4-4-5-5) sts at beg of row, purl to end, 11 (17-16-19-23-25) sts rem.

Dec 1 st at neck edge on following 2 (5-6-8-8-10) rows, then cont working neck edge even, *at the same time* cont to shape raglan edge as follows:

Dec 1 st at raglan edge on next 5 (2-4-3-1-3) RS rows. Then dec 1 st at raglan edge on every row 2 (8-4-6-12-10) times, 2 sts rem, k2tog, break off yarn and draw through loop.

Return to sts on spare needle, slip center 14 (16-16-18-18-20) sts onto a st holder, rejoin yarn to rem 20 (26-26-29-34-36) sts and knit to last 3 sts, k2tog, k1. Work WS row even.

RS row: BO 4 sts at beg of row, knit to last 3 sts, k2tog, k1. Work WS row even.

Next RS row: BO 3 (3-4-4-5-5) sts at beg of row, knit to last 3 sts, k2tog, k1, 11 (17-16-19-23-25) sts rem.

Now dec 1 st at neck edge on following 2 (5-6-8-8-10) rows, then cont working neck edge even, *at the same time* cont to shape raglan edge as follows:

Dec 1 st at raglan edge on next 5 (2-4-3-1-3) RS rows. Then dec 1 st at raglan edge on every row 2 (8-4-6-12-10) times, 2 sts rem, k2tog, break off yarn and draw through loop.

## Sleeve (Make 2)

Using size 6 [4mm] needles and M/C, cast on 63 sts.

## Back

Using size 6 [4mm] needles and M/C, cast on 104 (118-124-132-142-150) sts. Work 4 rows in seed st.

Beg with a knit row, work in St st throughout until Back measures 13 (13.5-14-14.5-15-15.5)" [33 (34.5-35.5-37-38-39.5)cm] from beg, end with RS row facing for next row.

SHAPE RAGLANS AS FOLLOWS (SEE NOTE ON DEC)
BO 4 sts at beg of next 4 rows. Then dec 1 st at each end of RS rows 24 (21-26-25-23-26) times, 40 (60-56-66-80-82) sts rem.

Dec 1 st at each end of every row 4 (10-6-8-14-12) times, 32 (40-44-50-52-58) sts rem. Place these sts on a stitch holder for back neck.

## Front

Work as given for Back until beg of raglan shaping.

SHAPE RAGLANS AS FOLLOWS (SEE NOTE ON DECS)
BO 4 sts at beg of next 4 rows. Then dec 1 st at each end of following RS rows 17 (17-20-20-20-21) times, 54 (68-68-76-86-92) sts rem. Work WS row even.

**Foundation row:** *K1, p1; rep from * to last st, k1.

**RS eyelet row:** K1, *YO, k2tog; rep from * to end. Purl next row, inc 1 st on this row, 64 sts.

PLACE FAIR ISLE PATT
AS FOLLOWS
**RS row:** Following Row 1 and beg at RHS of chart, work 8 st patt rep 8 times across row.

**WS row:** Following Row 2 and beg at LHS of chart, work 8 st patt rep 8 times across row.

Fair Isle patt is now set, follow chart Rows 3–46, followed by Rows 1–46 twice more in sequence, changing colors as indicated, *at the same time* inc 1 st at each end of row 9 and every following 10 (10-8-8-6-6)th row 9 (9-12-12-10-17) times, 84 (84-90-90-86-100) sts. Work all inc sts in Fair Isle patt as appropriate.

**Size XL only:** Inc 1 st at each end of every 8th row 5 times, 96 sts.

**All sizes:** Work even until Sleeve measures 17 (17-17½-17½-17¾-18)" [43 (43-44.5-44.5-45-45.5)cm] from beg, end with RS row facing for next row.

SHAPE RAGLANS AS FOLLOWS
(SEE NOTE ON DEC)
Complete the third rep of chart, then cont using M/C only working in St st, *at the same time,* BO 4 sts at beg of next 4 rows, then dec 1 st at each end of RS rows 26 (26-29-29-30-32) times, 16 (16-16-16-20-20) sts rem. Leave these sts on a st holder.

## Finishing

Weave in all ends. Block all pieces to given dimensions.

Join all raglan seams.

Using circular size 6 [4mm] needle and M/C, with RS facing and beg at LH sleeve, knit across 16 (16-16-16-20-20) sts from LH sleeve st holder, then pick up and knit 23 (23-25-25-25-25) sts down left front neck, knit across 14 (16-16-18-18-20) sts from front neck st holder, pick up and knit 23 (23-25-25-25-25) sts up right front neck, knit across 16 (16-16-16-20-20) sts from RH sleeve st holder, and knit across 32 (40-44-50-52-58) sts from back neck st holder, 124 (134-142-150-160-168) sts total. Knit 1 rnd inc 1 st at CB, 125 (135-143-151-161-169) sts.

**Eyelet rnd (RS):** K1, *YO, k2tog, repeat from * to end.

Knit 2 rnds. BO all sts knitwise.

Join side and Sleeve seams.

Using crochet hook and Color C, make the following cords:

1 x 150 chains for neckline, 2 x 120 chains for lower edge of Sleeves, 6 x 90 chains for Sleeves.

Using longest cord, thread through eyelet row at neckline. Using shortest cords, thread through eyelet rows on Sleeves. Using rem cords, thread through eyelet rows around lower edges of Sleeves. Thread cords in and out at neckline and on Sleeves, and whipping over the edges around lower edges of Sleeves.

Press lightly, following the instructions on the yarn label.

## well dressing

Well dressing is a springtime tradition where scenes are fashioned by setting flower petals into boards covered with clay. These boards are then used to decorate the town's well. Many towns in Derbyshire, England take part in the festival. Its origins are much debated: it's believed to date back to pagan times when the water gods would have been honored, but the custom has certainly been practiced continuously since the seventeenth century. Nowadays, this particular form of celebration is supposedly unique to the area, making well dressing into a tourist attraction. The local people now rejoice in the flow of both commerce and water into their towns.

# waves

## WOMEN'S CABLE AND FAIR ISLE SWEATER

The movement of water at the shore can vary between soft ripples and giant crashing waves. It is very seldom still and quiet, and because it's constantly changing, water has the ability to surprise us.

This simple-shaped, easy-to-wear sweater is created with classic patterns used in new and unexpected ways. The placement of the cables and the contraction of the fabric when working them causes the lower edges to ripple and wave. The asymmetry of the Fair Isle pattern used at the yoke, as well as the indistinct lines of simple striping of just two colors on a white ground creates the visual effect of tossing waves.

### Sizes/Finished Chest Measurements

S 34½" [87.5cm]

M 39" [99cm]

L 43" [109cm]

XL 47½" [120.5cm]

2X 51½" [131cm]

Instructions are given for the smallest size. If changes are necessary for larger sizes, the instructions are given in ( ). Where there is only one set of figures, this applies to all sizes.

### Materials

Extra by Needful Yarns (100% merino wool; 99yds [90m]/50g ball)

M/C, shade 2950: 15 (17-19-21-24) balls

Color A, shade 100: 3 (3-4-4-5) balls

Color B, shade 2001: 2 (2-2-3-3) balls

Color C, shade 2004: 2 (2-2-2-3) balls

Pair of size 8 [5mm] needles, size 8 [5mm] and size 7 [4.5mm] circular needles (both 16" [40.5cm] long) for neckline, cable needle, 2 stitch holders

Yarn amounts given are based on average requirements and are approximate.

### Gauge

22 sts and 22 rows = 4" [10cm] over Fair Isle patt on size 8 [5mm] needles

30 sts and 24 rows = 4" [10cm] over cable patt on size 8 [5mm] needles

One cable patt rep measures 2" [5cm] wide × 3" [7.5cm] long at lowest point.

Take the time to check your gauge; change the needle size if necessary to obtain the correct gauge and garment size.

REFER TO TECHNIQUES ON PAGE 18 FOR: **Cables**

REFER TO GLOSSARY ON PAGE 23 FOR: **Garter Ridge, Garter Stitch**

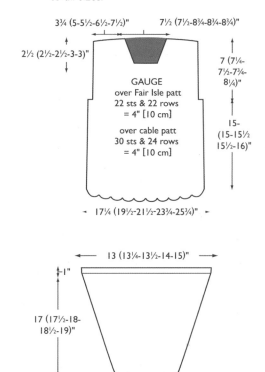

3¾ (5-5½-6½-7½)"     7½ (7½-8¾-8¾-8¾)"

2½ (2½-2½-3-3)"

7 (7¼-7½-7¾-8¼)"

GAUGE
over Fair Isle patt
22 sts & 22 rows
= 4" [10 cm]

over cable patt
30 sts & 24 rows
= 4" [10 cm]

15-(15-15½-15½-16)"

17¼ (19½-21½-23¾-25¾)"

13 (13¼-13½-14-15)"

1"

17 (17½-18-18½-19)"

9¼"

**Chart A**

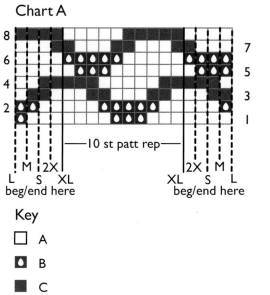

—10 st patt rep—

M 2X | 2X M
L S XL | XL S L
beg/end here | beg/end here

**Chart B**

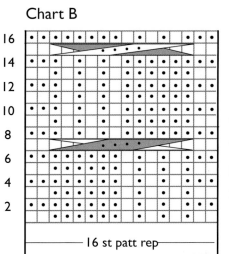

—16 st patt rep—

Charts read from R to L on RS rows,
and from L to R on WS rows.

**Key**

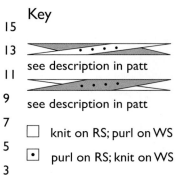

see description in patt

see description in patt

☐ knit on RS; purl on WS

• purl on RS; knit on WS

**Key**

☐ A

◖ B

■ C

## Cable Pattern
## Chart B (16 St Patt Rep)

Row 1 (RS): *K2, (p1, k1) 3 times, p6, k2; rep from * to end.

Row 2: *K8, (p1, k1) 3 times, k2; rep from * to end.

Rows 3–6: Rep Rows 1 and 2 twice more.

Row 7: *K2, sl next 7 sts onto CN and hold at back of work, purl next 5 sts from LH needle, (p1, k1) 3 times, p1 (7 sts from CN), k2; rep from * to end.

Row 8: *K3, (p1, k1) 3 times, k7; rep from * to end.

Row 9: *K2, p6, (k1, p1) 3 times, k2, rep from * to end.

Rows 10–14: Rep Rows 8 and 9 twice more, plus Row 8 once more.

Row 15: *K2, sl next 5 sts onto CN and hold at back of work, (p1, k1) 3 times, p1, then p5 sts from CN, k2; rep from * to end.

Row 16: Rep Row 2.

Rep Rows 1–16 for patt.

## Back

Using size 8 [5mm] needles and M/C, cast on 130 (146-162-178-194) sts. Knit 1 row.

PLACE CABLE PATTERN AS FOLLOWS:
RS row: K1, following Row 1 of Cable Patt, work 16 st patt rep 8 (9-10-11-12) times, k1.

*NOTE: place marker to indicate RS of fabric.*

WS row: K1, following Row 2 of Cable Patt, work 16 st patt rep 8 (9-10-11-12) times, k1.

Work following Cable Patt rows in sequence as set until Back measures 15 (15-15½-15½-16)" [38 (38-39.5-39.5-40.5)cm] from beg, take measurement at side seam at highest point on wavy edge, end with RS row facing for next row.

RS row: Using Color B, knit across row dec 36 (40-45-49-54) sts as follows:

K2 (4-2-4-2), * k2, (k2tog) 4 times, k8, (k2tog) 5 times, k4; rep from * 3 (3-4-4-5) more times, 0 (14-0-14-0) sts rem, k0 (2-0-2-0), (k2tog) 0 (4-0-4-0) times, k0 (4-0-4-0), 94 (106-117-129-140) sts rem.

WS row: Knit all sts. L and XL sizes only inc 1 st in center of row to bring st count to an even number, 94 (106-118-130-140) sts.

SHAPE ARMHOLES AS FOLLOWS:
Next 2 rows: Using Color C, BO 5 (5-5-5-4) sts at beg of each row, knit to end (forms garter ridge), 84 (96-108-120-132) sts rem.

PLACE FAIR ISLE PATT AS FOLLOWS:
RS row: Following Row 1 Chart A, beg at RHS of chart work first 2 (3-4-0-1) sts as shown, then work 10 st patt rep 8 (9-10-12-13) times across row, 2 (3-4-0-1) sts rem, work as shown at LHS of chart.

WS row: Following Row 2 Chart A, beg at LHS of chart, work first 2 (3-4-0-1) sts as shown, then work 10 st patt rep 8 (9-10-12-13) times, 2 (3-4-0-1) sts rem, work as shown at RHS of chart.

Work in Fair Isle patt as set, following chart rows in sequence and changing colors as indicated until Armhole measures 7 (7¼-7½-7¾-8¼)" [18 (18.5-19-19.5-21)cm] from beg of shaping, end with RS row facing for next row.

SHAPE SHOULDERS AS FOLLOWS:
Cont in patt, BO 7 (9-10-12-14) sts at beg of next 6 rows. Leave rem 42 (42-48-48-48) sts on a st holder for back neck.

## Front

Work as given for Back until Fair Isle patt has been placed.

Work even in patt until Armhole measures 4½ (4¾-5-4¾-5¼)"

[11.5 (12-12.5-12-13)cm] from beg of shaping, end with RS row facing for next row.

### SHAPE FRONT NECK AS FOLLOWS:
Work in patt across 31 (37-40-48-54) sts, turn (this is neck edge). Leave rem 53 (59-68-72-78) sts on a spare needle. Working on the 31 (37-40-48-54) sts only, dec 1 st at neck edge on following 10 (10-10-12-12) rows, 21 (27-30-36-42) sts rem. Work even until Front measures the same as Back before shoulder shaping, end with RS row facing for next row.

### SHAPE LH SHOULDER AS FOLLOWS:
Cont in patt, BO 7 (9-10-12-14) sts at beg of next row. Work WS row even.

Rep last 2 rows. BO rem 7 (9-10-12-14) sts.

Return to sts on spare needle. Slip center 22 (22-28-24-24) sts onto a st holder for front neck. Rejoin yarn to rem 31 (37-40-48-54) sts and work in patt to end. Dec 1 st at neck edge on following 10 (10-10-12-12) rows, 21 (27-30-36-42) sts rem. Work even until Front measures the same as the Back before shoulder shaping, end with WS row facing for next row.

### SHAPE RH SHOULDER AS FOLLOWS:
Cont in patt, BO 7 (9-10-12-14) sts at beg of row. Work RS row even.

Rep last 2 rows. BO rem 7 (9-10-12-14) sts.

## Sleeve (Make 2)

Using size 8 [5mm] needles and M/C, cast on 70 sts. Knit 1 row.

### PLACE CABLE PATTERN AS FOLLOWS:
RS row: K3, work Row 1 of Cable Patt 4 times, k3.

*NOTE: place marker to indicate RS of fabric.*

WS row: K3, work Row 2 of Cable Patt 4 times, k3.

Work in Cable Patt as set, following rows in sequence, *at the same time* inc 1 st at each end of row 5 and every following 6th row 1 (2-4-7-15) time, 74 (76-80-86-102) sts. Then inc 1 st at each end of every 8 (8-8-8-4)th row 10 (10-9-7-3) times, 94 (96-98-100-108) sts, work all inc sts in garter stitch (knit every row).

Work even until Sleeve measures 17 (17½-18-18½-19)" [43 (44.5-45.5-47-48.5)cm], from cast-on edge, taking measurement at highest point on wavy edge. End with RS row facing for next row. Place marker at each end of this row.

Cont even in patt for another 1" [2.5cm], end with RS row facing for next row.

Next row: Dec 6 sts across top of each cable section by working k2tog 6 times, 70 (72-74-76-84) sts rem. BO all sts loosely.

## Finishing and Neck

Weave in all ends. Block all pieces to given dimensions.

Join both shoulder seams.

Using size 8 [5mm] circular needle and Color A, with RS facing beg at LH shoulder seam, pick up and knit 18 (20-20-22-24) sts down left front neck, knit across 22 (22-28-24-24) sts from front neck st holder, then pick up and knit 18 (20-20-22-24) sts up right front neck, knit across 42 (42-48-48-48) sts from back neck st holder, 100 (104-116-116-120) sts total, join in the rnd.

Change to Color B, knit 1 rnd, purl 1 rnd (garter ridge).

Change back to Color A, knit 2 rnds (St st).

Change to size 7 [4.5mm] circular needle and Color C, knit 1 rnd, purl 1 rnd.

Change back to Color A, knit 2 rnds, dec 7 sts evenly on second rnd, 93 (97-109-109-113) sts rem.

Change back to Color B, knit 1 rnd, purl 1 rnd.

Change back to Color A, knit 4 rnds.

Change to size 8 [5mm] circular needle, knit 1 rnd inc 7 sts evenly across rnd, 100 (104-116-116-120) sts. Knit 1 rnd. BO all sts loosely.

Allow neck to turn down at second Color B garter ridge and stitch BO edge to pick-up row on WS of garment.

Set in Sleeves to armholes, matching top of Sleeve above marker to BO sts on body. Sew side and Sleeve seams.

Press lightly, following the instructions on the yarn label.

## the wave

The depiction of the elements has been an enduring theme for artists working in all mediums. They strive to capture transitory moments of beauty—a snowy landscape, trees swaying in the wind, subtle changes in sunlight or the crashing of waves. Japanese artist Hokusai (1760–1849) achieves just that in the woodblock print *The Great Wave at Kanagawa.* Works such as this one grew out of a tradition of Japanese artists attempting to express the beauty present in every passing moment.

# spindrift

## SUMMER TANK

Bodies of water vary greatly in size and depth, from the large expanse of an ocean to deep glacial lakes, to trickling brooks. Waterscapes delight us, and the moods they provoke are as diverse as the sources themselves.

This shimmering summer tank incorporates a softly rippling lower edge and a wave-patterned Fair Isle band to evoke a feeling of bubbling streams and rivers. To allude to water's reflective qualities, a high-sheen yarn was chosen. Then, to heighten this effect, a carry-along yarn, with tiny mirrors along its length, is added at the lower edge, creating a garment that shimmers in the light.

### Sizes/Finished Chest Measurements

XS 32" [81cm]

S 37" [94cm]

M 39" [99cm]

L 42" [106.5cm]

XL 46" [117cm]

2X 49" [124.5cm]

Instructions are given for the smallest size. If changes are necessary for larger sizes, the instructions are given in ( ). Where there is only one set of figures, this applies to all sizes.

### Materials

Cotton Twist by Berroco (70% mercerized cotton, 30% rayon; 85yds [78m]/50g skein).

M/C, shade 8368: 5 (5-6-7-9) skeins

Color A, shade 8358: 1 (1-2-2-3) skein

Color B, shade 8337: 1 (1-2-2-2) skein

Color C, shade 8301: 1 (1-1-2-2) skein

Mirror FX by Berroco (100% polyester; 60yds [55m]/10g ball) shade 9002: 1 ball for all sizes

Pair each of size 8 [5mm] needles and size 9 [5.5mm] needles, size 8 [5mm] circular needle (16" [40.5cm] long), 4 stitch holders, size G/6 [4mm] crochet hook, six ¾" [2cm] diameter plastic rings, six ¾" [2cm] diameter sequins

Yarn amounts are based on average requirements and are approximate.

### Gauge

20 sts and 23 rows = 4" [10cm] over St st on size 8 [5mm] needles

Take time to check your gauge; change the needle sizes if necessary to obtain the correct gauge and garment size.

REFER TO TECHNIQUES ON PAGE 18 FOR: Buttonhole Stitch, Crochet Chain, Short Rows, 3-Needle Bind-Off

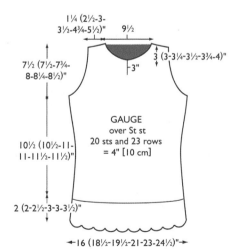

1¼ (2½-3-3½-4¾-5½)"          9½

7½ (7½-7¾-8-8¼-8½)"

3 (3-3¼-3½-3¾-4)"

3"

GAUGE
over St st
20 sts and 23 rows
= 4" [10 cm]

10½ (10½-11-11-11½-11½)"

2 (2-2½-3-3-3½)"

16 (18½-19½-21-23-24½)"

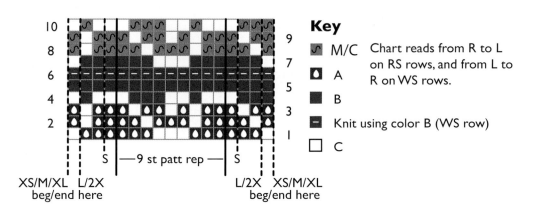

**Key**

| | | |
|---|---|---|
| ∿ | M/C | Chart reads from R to L on RS rows, and from L to R on WS rows. |
| ◖ | A | |
| ▪ | B | |
| – | Knit using color B (WS row) | |
| ☐ | C | |

S —9 st patt rep— S

XS/M/XL  L/2X          L/2X  XS/M/XL
beg/end here            beg/end here

## Back

Using size 8 [5mm] needles and Color B, cast on 80 (92-98-104-116-122) sts.

Add Mirror FX yarn, carrying it along with Color B, knit 1 row.

Change to Color A and Mirror FX, and work 1 row in Feather and Fan patt as follows:

(RS) XS, S, L, XL sizes: K2, YO, k2tog, *(k2tog) twice, (YO, k1) 4 times, (k2tog) twice, rep from * to last 4 sts, k2tog, YO, k2.

(RS) M and 2X sizes: K1, *(k2tog) twice, (YO, k1) 4 times, (k2tog) twice, rep from * to last st, k1.

Break off Mirror FX and cont using Color A only.

WS rows: All sizes, purl all sts.

RS rows: Work as RS given above for size.

Rep the last 2 rows 5 (5-6-7-7-8) more times, plus WS row once more, inc 1 st for sizes L and 2X only on last row, 80 (92-98-105-116-123) sts.

Change to size 9 [5.5mm] needles.

PLACE FAIR ISLE PATT AS FOLLOWS:
RS row: Following Row 1 of chart, beg at RHS of chart, work first 4 (1-4-3-4-3) sts as shown, then work 9 st patt rep 8 (10-10-11-12-13) times, 4 (1-4-3-4-3) sts rem, work these as shown at LHS of chart.

WS row: Following Row 2 of chart, beg at LHS of chart, work first 4 (1-4-3-4-3) sts as shown, then work 9 st patt rep 8 (10-10-11-12-13) times, 4 (1-4-3-4-3) sts rem, work these as shown at RHS of chart.

Work Rows 3 and 4 of chart as set, changing colors as indicated.

Rows 5 and 6 work according to chart using Color B plus Mirror FX. Break off Mirror FX at end of Row 6.

Cont working Rows 7–10 of chart as set, changing colors as indicated.

Change to size 8 [5mm] needles and M/C, beg with a knit row, work 2 rows in St st, dec 1 st for sizes L and 2X only on first row, 80 (92-98-104-116-122) sts.

SHAPE WAIST AS FOLLOWS:
Cont in St st throughout, dec 1 st at each end of next row. Work 3 rows even.

Rep the last 4 rows 2 more times, plus the dec row once more, 72 (84-90-96-108-114) sts rem.

Work 5 rows even.

Inc 1 st at each end of next row. Work 3 rows even. Rep the last 4 rows 2 more times, plus the inc row once more, 80 (92-98-104-116-122) sts.

Work even in St st until Back measures 12½ (12½-13½-14-14½-15)" [32 (32-34.5-35.5-37-38)cm] from cast-on edge (measuring from highest point of scallop edge), end with RS row facing for next row.

SHAPE ARMHOLES AS FOLLOWS:
BO 4 sts at beg of next 2 rows, and 2 sts at beg of following 2 rows. Dec 1 st at each end of next 4 rows, 60 (72-78-84-96-102) sts rem.

Work even in St st until Armhole measures 6½ (6½-6¾-7-7¼-7½)" [16.5 (16.5-17-18-18.5-19)cm] from beg of shaping, end with RS row facing for next row.

SHAPE BACK NECK AS FOLLOWS:
K11 (17-20-23-29-32), turn (this is neck edge). Leave rem 49 (55-58-61-67-70) sts on a spare needle. Dec 1 st at neck edge on next 5 rows, 6 (12-15-18-24-27) sts rem. Work RS row even.

SHAPE RIGHT SHOULDER AS FOLLOWS:
WS row: Working in short rows, work to last 2 (4-5-6-8-9) sts, wrap next st, turn. Work RS row even.

Next WS row: Work to last 4 (8-10-12-16-18) sts, wrap next st, turn. Work RS row even. Work across all sts, working the wrap tog with the st it wraps. Place these 6 (12-15-18-24-27) sts on a stitch holder.

Return to sts on spare needle. Rejoin yarn and BO center 38 sts, knit rem 11 (17-20-23-29-32) sts. Dec 1 st at neck edge on next 5 rows, 6 (12-15-18-24-27) sts rem.

SHAPE LEFT SHOULDER AS FOLLOWS:
RS row: Working in short rows, work to last 2 (4-5-6-8-9) sts, wrap next st, turn. Work WS row even.

Next RS row: Work to last 4 (8-10-12-16-18) sts, wrap next st, turn. Work WS row even.

Work across all sts, working the wrap tog with the st it wraps. Place these 6 (12-15-18-24-27) sts onto another stitch holder.

## Front

Work as given for Back until armhole shaping is complete.

DIVIDE FOR FRONT NECK OPENING AS FOLLOWS:
RS row: Work across 28 (34-37-40-46-49) sts, k2tog, turn (this is CF opening). Leave rem 30 (36-39-42-48-51) sts on a spare needle for RHS front.

Work even on the 29 (35-38-41-47-50) sts until CF opening measures 3" [7.5cm], end with a WS row facing for next row.

SHAPE LHS FRONT NECK AS FOLLOWS:
BO 6 sts at beg of next row. Work RS row even. Rep last 2 rows once more. Now dec 1 st at neck edge on next 11 rows, 6 (12-15-18-24-27) sts rem. Work even on these sts until Front measures the same as the Back before the shoulder shaping, end with WS row facing for next row.

SHAPE SHOULDER AS FOLLOWS:
Working in short rows, work to last 2 (4-5-6-8-9) sts, wrap next st, turn. Work RS row even.

Next WS row: Work to last 4 (8-10-12-16-18) sts, wrap next st, turn. Work RS row even.

Work across all sts, working the wrap tog with the st it wraps. Place these 6 (12-15-18-24-27) sts onto a stitch holder.

Return to sts on spare needle, rejoin yarn, k2tog, work to end.

Work even on the 29 (35-38-41-47-50) sts until CF opening measures 3" [7.5cm], end with RS row facing for next row.

SHAPE RHS FRONT NECK AS FOLLOWS:
BO 6 sts at beg of next row. Work WS row even. Rep last 2 rows once more. Now dec 1 st at neck edge on next 11 rows, 6 (12-15-18-24-27) sts rem. Work even on these sts until Front measures the same as the Back before the shoulder shaping, end with RS row facing for next row.

SHAPE SHOULDER AS FOLLOWS:
Working in short rows, work to last 2 (4-5-6-8-9) sts, wrap next st, turn. Work WS row even.

Next RS row: Work to last 4 (8-10-12-16-18) sts, wrap next st, turn. Work WS row even.

Work across all sts, working the wrap tog with the st it wraps. Place these 6 (12-15-18-24-27) sts onto another stitch holder.

## Finishing

Sew in all ends. Block pieces to given measurements.

Join both shoulder seams using the 3-needle bind-off method.

Using circular size 8 [5mm] needle and Color B with RS facing, pick up and knit 15 sts down each side of CF opening. BO all sts knitwise.

Using circular size 8 [5mm] needle and Color B with RS facing, beg at top of CF opening (RHS), pick up and knit 29 (29-31-33-35-37) sts up RHS front neck, 9 sts down RHS back neck, 33 sts across back neck, 9 sts up LHS back neck, and 29 (29-31-33-35-37) sts down LHS front neck, 109 (109-113-117-121-125) sts total. Knit 1 row. BO all sts knitwise.

Using size 8 [5mm] needles and Color B, with RS facing, pick up 82 (82-86-90-94-98) sts around armhole. BO all sts knitwise.

Rep for second armhole.

Join side seams.

Using crochet hook and Color B, make 2 crochet cords 50 chains long (approx 8" [20.5cm]), work single crochet into each chain and attach each cord to top of CF opening.

Using Color B, cover each of the rings using buttonhole stitch. Attach a sequin to the back of each ring. Stitch 3 rings together and then sew to end of crochet cords.

Press lightly, following the instructions on the yarn label.

# the indian festival of holi

There are many festivals the world over that celebrate the end of winter and the beginning of spring in a fun and frivolous way—Mardi Gras, Carnival, and the Indian festival of Holi.

Holi, a Hindu festival, lasts several days and is known as the color festival because it involves the throwing and spraying of color. It is held at the time of the full moon occurring at the end of February or beginning of March. On the eve of the festival, spring cleaning is carried out and old belongings are burnt on bonfires. This symbolizes that it still is winter and warmth is needed. The following day is considered spring, requiring cooling. Water is mixed with bright shades of pink, green, and saffron (traditionally made from steeping flowers). This colored water is indiscriminately sprayed at people; no one who is in the street will escape the dousing.

# crystal

## CLASSIC FAIR ISLE TURTLENECK

Water exists in our world in different states. It is most common as a flowing liquid, but can also be a misty vapor or frozen solid into ice crystals or snowflakes.

As a traditional Fair Isle pattern, the snowflake can be found in different forms—as a classic horizontal striped band or as a sporty oversized single motif. Here, for added interest when knitting the pattern, and to represent the slippery characteristics of water in its frozen form, the snowflakes appear to be slipping out of a regular alignment or accumulating as they might during a snowstorm.

Strong pattern definition is achieved by setting icy white and lilac against a midnight-sky navy. The overall look is reminiscent of a frosty evening where the snow might crunch underfoot as snowflakes flutter down to Earth.

### Sizes/Finished Chest Measurements

S 32" [81cm]

M 37" [94cm]

L 42" [106.5cm]

XL 48" [122cm]

2X 53" [134.5cm]

Instructions are given for the smallest size. If changes are necessary for larger sizes, the instructions are given in ( ). Where there is only one set of figures, this applies to all sizes.

### Materials

Merino/Alpaca by SweaterKits (60% merino, 40% alpaca; 120yds [110m]/ 50g ball)

M/C, shade 06 Midnight Navy: 9 (9-10-12-13) balls

Color A, shade 01 White: 2 (2-2-2-3) balls

Color B, shade 09 Grape: 2 (2-2-2-3) balls

Pair each of size 7 [4.5mm], size 4 [3.5mm] and size 5 [3.75mm] needles, 2 stitch holders.

### Gauge

24 sts and 25 rows = 4" [10cm] over Fair Isle patt on size 7 [4.5mm] needles

20 sts and 28 rows = 4" [10cm] over St st on size 5 [3.75mm] needles

Take the time to check your gauge; change the needle size if necessary to obtain the correct gauge and garment size.

REFER TO GLOSSARY ON PAGE 23 FOR: **Seed Stitch**

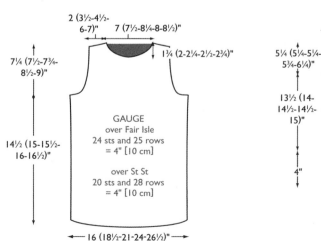

2 (3½-4½-6-7)"

7 (7½-8¼-8-8½)"

7¼ (7½-7¾-8½-9)"

1¾ (2-2¼-2½-2¾)"

GAUGE
over Fair Isle
24 sts and 25 rows
= 4" [10 cm]

over St St
20 sts and 28 rows
= 4" [10 cm]

14½ (15-15½-16-16½)"

16 (18½-21-24-26½)"

13 (13½-14-15½-16½)"

5¼ (5¼-5¼-5¾-6¼)"

13½ (14-14½-14½-15)"

4"

10"

## Chart A

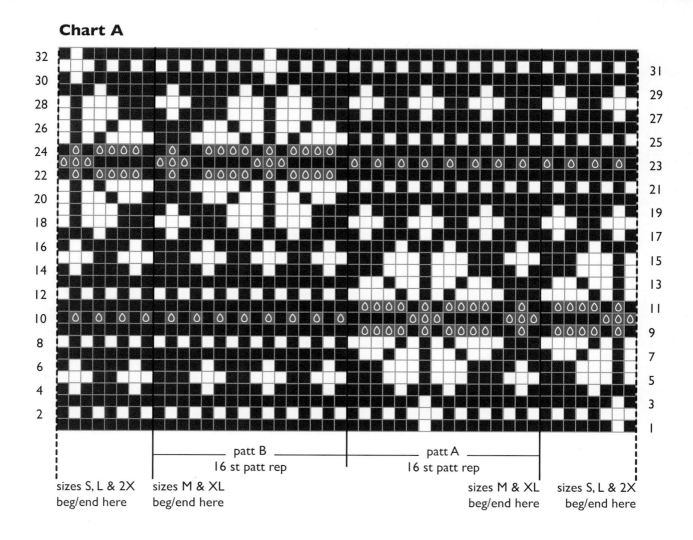

patt B
16 st patt rep

patt A
16 st patt rep

sizes S, L & 2X
beg/end here

sizes M & XL
beg/end here

sizes M & XL
beg/end here

sizes S, L & 2X
beg/end here

### Key

■ M/C

□ A

 B

Chart reads from R to L on RS rows,
and from L to R on WS rows.

## Back

Using size 7 [4.5mm] needles and M/C, cast on 92 (108-124-140-156) sts, work 3 rows in seed st, inc 4 sts evenly across last row, 96 (112-128-144-160) sts.

PLACE FAIR ISLE PATT AS FOLLOWS:

Row 1 (RS): Following Row 1 Chart A, work first 8 (0-8-0-8) sts as shown at RHS of chart, then work 16 st rep Patt A 3 (4-4-5-5) times, followed by 16 st rep Patt B 2 (3-3-4-4) times, 8 (0-8-0-8) sts rem, work these as shown at LHS of chart.

Row 2: Following Row 2 Chart A, work first 8 (0-8-0-8) sts as shown at LHS of chart, then work 16 st rep Patt B 2 (3-3-4-4) times, followed by 16 st rep Patt A 3 (4-4-5-5) times, 8 (0-8-0-8) sts rem, work these as shown at RHS of chart.

Cont working Chart A rows in sequence as set until Back measures 14½ (15-15½-16-16½)" [37 (38-39.5-40.5-42)cm] from beg, end with RS row facing for next row.

SHAPE ARMHOLES AS FOLLOWS:
Keeping continuity of patt, BO 4 sts at beg of next 4 rows. Then dec 1 st at each end of following 4 rows, 72 (88-104-120-136) sts rem.

Cont working even in patt until armhole measures 7¼ (7½-7¾-8½-9)" [18.5 (19-19.5-21.5-23)cm] from beg of shaping, end with RS row facing for next row.

SHAPE SHOULDERS AS FOLLOWS:
Cont in patt BO 5 (7-9-12-14) sts at beg of next 6 rows. Leave rem 42 (46-50-48-52) sts on a stitch holder.

## Front

Using size 7 [4.5mm] needles and M/C, cast on 92 (108-124-140-156) sts, work 3 rows in seed st, inc 4 sts evenly across last row, 96 (112-128-144-160) sts.

## Chart B

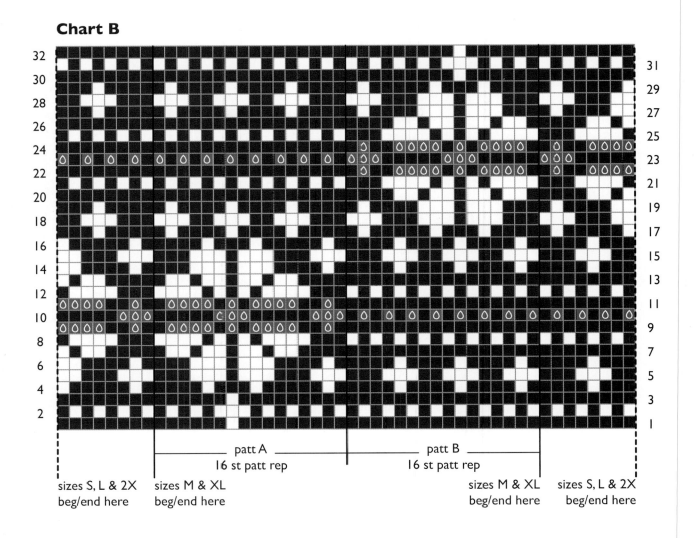

sizes S, L & 2X
beg/end here

sizes M & XL
beg/end here

patt A
16 st patt rep

patt B
16 st patt rep

sizes M & XL
beg/end here

sizes S, L & 2X
beg/end here

## Key

■ M/C

□ A

 B

Chart reads from R to L on RS rows,
and from L to R on WS rows.

PLACE FAIR ISLE PATT AS
FOLLOWS:

Row 1 (RS): Following Row 1 Chart B,
work first 8 (0-8-0-8) sts as shown at
RHS of chart, then work 16 st rep Patt
B 2 (3-3-4-4) times, followed by 16 st
rep Patt A 3 (4-4-5-5) times, 8 (0-8-0-
8) sts rem, work these as shown at
LHS of chart.

Row 2: Following Row 2 Chart B,
work first 8 (0-8-0-8) sts as shown at
LHS of chart, then work 16 st rep Patt
A 3 (4-4-5-5) times, followed by 16 st
patt rep Patt B 2 (3-3-4-4) times, 8 (0-
8-0-8) sts rem, work these as shown at
RHS of chart.

Cont working Chart B rows in sequence

as now set until Front measures 14½
(15-15½-16-16½)" [37 (38-39.5-40.5-
42)cm] from beg, end with RS row
facing for next row.

Shape armholes as given for Back, 72
(88-104-120-136) sts rem.

Cont working even in patt until armhole measures 5½ (5½-5½-6-6¼)"
[14 (14-14-15-16)cm] from beg of
shaping, end with RS row facing for
next row.

SHAPE FRONT NECK AS FOLLOWS:
Work across 21 (28-36-44-51) sts in
patt, turn (this is neck edge). Leave
rem 51 (60-68-76-85) sts on a spare
needle. Working on the 21 (28-36-44-

51) sts only, cont in patt, dec 1 st at
neck edge on next 6 (7-9-8-9) rows, 15
(21-27-36-42) sts rem. Work even in
patt until armhole measures the same
as Back before shoulder shaping, end
with RS row facing for next row.

SHAPE LH SHOULDER AS FOLLOWS:
BO 5 (7-9-12-14) sts at beg of row,
work in patt to end. Work WS row
even in patt. Rep these 2 rows once
more. BO rem 5 (7-9-12-14) sts.

Return to sts on spare needle. Slip
center 30 (32-32-32-34) sts onto a
stitch holder. Rejoin yarn and work in
patt to end. Dec 1 st at neck edge on
next 6 (7-9-8-9) rows, 15 (21-27-36-

42) sts rem. Work even in patt until armhole measures the same as Back before shoulder shaping, end with WS row facing for next row.

SHAPE RH SHOULDER AS FOLLOWS:
BO 5 (7-9-12-14) sts at beg of row, work in patt to end. Work RS row even in patt. Rep these 2 rows once more. BO rem 5 (7-9-12-14) sts.

## Sleeve (Make 2)

Using size 4 [3.5mm] needles and M/C, cast on 50 sts.

RS row: (P2, k2); rep to last 2 sts, p2.

WS row: (K2, p2); rep to last 2 sts, k2.

Rep these 2 rows until Sleeve measures 4" [10cm], ending with a WS row.

Change to size 5 [3.75mm] needles and beg with a knit row, work in St st throughout, *at the same time* inc 1 st at each end of next row and then every following 12 (12-10-8-8)th row 7 (4-9-9-5) times, 66 (60-70-70-62) sts, then inc 1 st at each end of every following 0 (10-0-6-6)th row 0 (4-0-4-10) times, 66 (68-70-78-82) sts. Cont working even until Sleeve measures 17.5 (18-18.5-18.5-19)" [44.5 (45.5-47-47-48.5)cm] from beg, end with RS row facing for next row.

SHAPE SLEEVE CAP AS FOLLOWS:
Cont in St st, BO 4 sts at beg of next 2 rows and 2 sts at beg of following 2 rows, 54 (56-58-66-70) sts. Then dec 1 st at each end of next and every following RS row 14 (14-14-15-16) times, 24 (26-28-34-36) sts rem. BO 3 (3-4-5-5) sts at beg of next 4 rows. BO rem 12 (14-12-14-16) sts.

## Finishing and Turtleneck

Weave in all ends. Block out all pieces to given dimensions.

Join RH shoulder seam.

Using size 4 [3.5mm] needles and M/C, with RS facing and beg at LH shoulder, pick up and knit 14 (15-15-18-17) sts down left front neck, knit across 30 (32-32-32-34) sts from front neck st holder, pick up and knit 14 (15-15-18-17) sts up right front neck, and knit across 42 (46-50-48-52) sts from back neck st holder, 100 (108-112-116-120) sts total.

WS row: (K2, p2) to end.

RS row: Rep WS row.

Rep the last 2 rows 20 more times. BO all sts loosely in rib as set.

Join LHS shoulder. Join Turtleneck seam, reversing seam at halfway point for turn-back.

Set in Sleeves to armholes. Join side and Sleeve seams.

Press lightly, following the instructions on the yarn label.

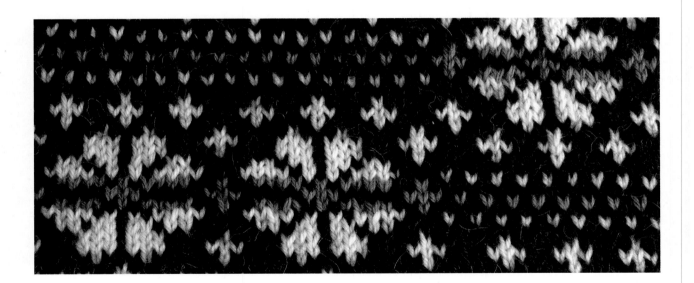

# the history of blue

Blue has always been a color associated with water. Nautical terms are used to describe specific shades of blue—navy blue and ultramarine blue—for example. The term for the latter shade, derived from the stone lapis lazuli, refers to European artists importing it from Afghanistan; the translation of the name is "from beyond the sea." The great expense incurred in obtaining this particular blue meant that it became linked with displays of wealth. Art patrons requested that it be used in their commissioned paintings, oftentimes religious scenes. Thus it became the color often used for the robes of the Virgin Mary, associating it with spirituality.

# ocean

## UNISEX CABLE AND FAIR ISLE SWEATER

Water has a cooling effect, but sometimes, out at sea, that can become a little too much of a good thing. The traditional sweaters worn by fishermen were designed to combat both the spray and the bracingly cool maritime breezes. These sweaters were made in stitches chosen to create dense fabric to prevent the harsh winds from reaching the skin.

Harking back to traditional seafaring garments, this sweater includes a cable stitch that ripples back and forth in a wavelike pattern. The graphic Fair Isle patterns suggest points on a compass or the directions of the winds. A blue-and-green palette was selected from hues found in the deep waters of the ocean. The sizing of the instructions allows it to be made for both men and women.

### Sizes/Finished Chest Measurements

S 39" [99cm]

M 42" [106.5cm]

L 46" [117cm]

XL 50" [127cm]

2X 53" [134.5cm]

Instructions are given for the smallest size. If changes are necessary for larger sizes, the instructions are given in ( ). Where there is only one set of figures, this applies to all sizes.

### Materials

1824 Wool by Mission Falls (100% wool; 85yds [78m]/50g ball)

M/C, Teal shade 030: 13 (14-16-18-19) balls

Color A, Denim shade 021: 5 (5-6-6-6) balls

Color B, Cornflower shade 020: 3 (3-3-4-4) balls

Color C, Aster shade 0536: 1 ball

Color D, Stone shade 002: 3 (3-4-4-5) balls

Color E, Sprout shade 0531: 2 (2-2-2-3) balls

Pair each of size 7 [4.5mm] needles, size 8 [5mm] needles, size 7 [4.5mm] circular needle (16" [40cm] long) for neckband, 1 stitch holder, size G/7 [4.5mm] crochet hook

Yarn amounts given are based on average requirements and are approximate.

### Gauge

18 sts and 21 rows = 4" [10cm] over Fair Isle patt on size 8 [5mm] needles

22 sts and 26 rows = 4" [10cm] over cable patt on size 7 [4.5mm] needles

Take the time to check your gauge; change the needle size if necessary to obtain the correct gauge and garment size.

REFER TO TECHNIQUES ON PAGE 18 FOR: Cables, Crochet Chain

REFER TO GLOSSARY ON PAGE 23 FOR: Seed Stitch

### Special Abbreviations

C4F: slip next 2 stitches onto cable needle and hold at front, knit 2 from left-hand needle, then knit 2 from cable needle.

C4B: slip next 2 stitches onto cable needle and hold at back, knit 2 from left-hand needle, then knit 2 from cable needle.

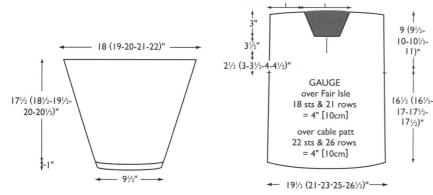

## Chart A

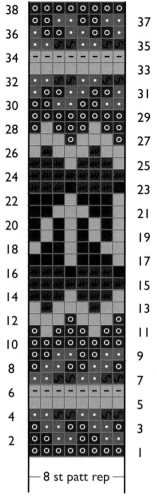

**Key**

- ■ M/C
- ◉ A
- ▣ B
- ⧆ C
- ▨ D
- – Knit using Color D (WS row)
- ▧ E

Work rows 1-38, then 11-28, then 1-28 for patt.

Chart reads from R to L on RS rows, and from L to R on WS rows.

— 8 st patt rep —

## Chart B

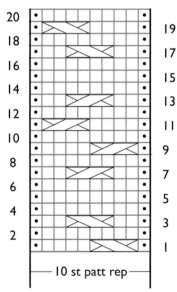

**Key**

- ⤬ C4B
- ⤬ C4F
- □ Knit on RS; purl on WS
- ⊡ Purl on RS; knit on WS

Chart reads from R to L on RS rows, and from L to R on WS rows.

— 10 st patt rep —

Cable Pattern
Chart B (10 St Patt Rep)
Row 1: P1, C4F, k4, p1.

Row 2 and all WS rows: K1, p8, k1.

Row 3: P1, k2, C4F, k2, p1.

Row 5: P1, k8, p1.

Row 7: P1, k2, C4B, k2, p1.

Row 9: P1, C4B, k4, p1.

Row 11: P1, k4, C4B, p1.

Row 13: P1, k2, C4B, k2, p1.

Row 15: Rep Row 5.

Row 17: Rep Row 3.

Row 19: P1, k4, C4F, p1.

Row 20: Rep Row 2.

Rep Rows 1–20 for patt.

### Back

Using size 8 [5mm] needles and Color A, cast on 78 (86-94-102-110) sts. Work 2 (2-6-8-8) rows in seed st, inc 10 sts evenly across last row, 88 (96-104-112-120) sts.

PLACE FAIR ISLE PATT AS FOLLOWS:
RS row: Following Row 1 Chart A, beg at RHS of chart, work 8 st patt rep 11 (12-13-14-15) times across row.

WS row: Following Row 2 Chart A, beg at LHS of chart, work 8 st patt rep 11 (12-13-14-15) times across row.

Work Rows 3–38 Chart A in sequence, changing colors as indicated. Then work Rows 11–28 Chart A. Then work Rows 1–28 Chart A; Back will now measure approx 16½ (16½-17-17½-17½)" [42 (42-43-44.5-44.5)cm], from cast-on edge, end with RS row facing for next row. Place markers at each end of last row to indicate position of armholes.

Change to size 7 [4.5mm] needles and using M/C, knit 1 row. Cont using M/C throughout.

WS row: Knit all sts inc 18 (20-22-24-26) evenly across row, 106 (116-126-136-146) sts.

PLACE CABLE PATT AS FOLLOWS:
RS row: P3, following Row 1 of Cable Patt, work 10 st patt rep 10 (11-12-13-14) times, 3 sts rem, p3.

WS row: K3, following Row 2 of Cable Patt, work 10 st patt rep 10 (11-12-13-14) times, 3 sts rem, k3.

Cable Patt is now set. Cont working Cable Patt rows in sequence until Back measures 9 (9½-10-10½-11)" [23 (24-25.5-26.5-28)cm] from arm-hole marker, end with RS row facing for next row.

SHAPE SHOULDERS AS FOLLOWS:
Cont in Cable Patt, BO 12 (13-14-15-17) sts at beg of next 6 rows. Leave rem 34 (38-42-46-44) sts on a stitch holder.

## Front

Work as given for Back until Cable Patt is set.

Cont using M/C throughout working Cable Patt rows in sequence until Front measures 2½ (3-3½-4-4½)" [6.5 (7.5-9-10-11.5)cm] from armhole marker.

DIVIDE FOR CF OPENING AS FOLLOWS:
Cont in Cable Patt, work across 53 (58-63-68-73) sts, join a second ball of M/C, work across rem 53 (58-63-68-73) sts in patt.

Cont working each side separately, using a different ball for each side:

WS row: Using ball #2, work 49 (54-59-64-69) sts in patt, p2tog, YO, k2. Using ball #1, k2, YO, p2tog, work in patt to end.

RS row: Using ball #1, work 51 (56-61-66-71) sts in patt, k2. Using ball #2, k2, work in patt to end.

Next WS row: Using ball #2, work 51 (56-61-66-71) sts in patt, k2. Using ball #1, k2, work in patt to end.

Rep the last 2 rows 7 more times, then rep RS row once more.

Next WS row: Using ball #2, work 49 (54-59-64-69) sts in patt, p2tog, YO, k2. Using ball #1, k2, YO, p2tog, work in patt to end.

Cont working each side separately in patt, knitting the last/first 2 sts before/after CF opening on every row as before, until CF opening measures 3½" [9cm], end with RS row facing for next row.

SHAPE LH FRONT NECK AS FOLLOWS:
Work in patt to CF, turn (this is neck edge). Leave rem sts on a spare needle for RHS.

WS row: BO 4 (4-4-5-5) sts at beg of row, work in patt to end. Work RS row even.

Next WS row: BO 4 (4-4-5-5) sts at beg of row, work in patt to end.

Cont in patt dec 1 st at neck edge on next 9 (11-13-13-12) rows, 36 (39-42-45-51) sts rem.

Work even until Front measures the same as Back before shoulder shaping, end with RS row facing for next row.

SHAPE LH SHOULDER AS FOLLOWS:
RS row: BO 12 (13-14-15-17) sts at beg of next row, work WS row even. Rep the last 2 rows once more. BO rem 12 (13-14-15-17) sts.

SHAPE RH FRONT NECK AS FOLLOWS:
Return to sts on spare needle.

RS row: BO 4 (4-4-5-5) sts at beg of row, work to end in patt. Work WS row even.

Next RS row: BO 4 (4-4-5-5) sts at beg of row, work to end in patt.

Cont in patt, dec 1 st at neck edge on next 9 (11-13-13-12) rows, 36 (39-42-45-51) sts rem.

Work even until Front measures the same as Back before shoulder shaping, end with WS row facing for next row.

SHAPE RH SHOULDER AS FOLLOWS:
WS row: BO 12 (13-14-15-17) sts at beg of next row, work RS row even. Rep the last 2 rows once more. BO rem 12 (13-14-15-17) sts.

## Sleeve (Make 2)

Using size 7 [4.5mm] needles and M/C, cast on 52 sts, work 2 rows in seed st.

WORK CABLE SETUP ROWS AS FOLLOWS:
RS row: (P2, k8) to last 2 sts, p2.

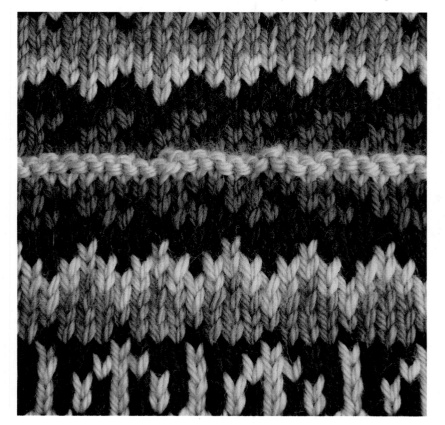

WS row: (K2, p8) to last 2 sts, k2.

Rep these 2 rows once more.

PLACE CABLE PATT AS FOLLOWS:
RS row: P1, m1 (by picking up strand between next 2 sts), following Row 1 of Cable Patt, work 10 st patt rep 5 times, 1 st rem, m1 as before, p1, 54 sts.

WS row: P1, k1, following Row 2 of Cable Patt, work 10 st patt rep 5 times, 2 sts rem, k1, p1.

Cable Patt is now set. Cont following Cable Patt rows in sequence as set, *at the same time* inc 1 st at each end of every following 4th row 9 (17-20-27-32) times, 72 (88-94-108-118) sts.

Then inc 1 st at each end of every 6th row 12 (7-6-2-0) times, 96 (102-106-112-118) sts, work all inc sts into Cable Patt as appropriate. Work even in patt until Sleeve measures 18.5 (19½-20½-21-21½)" [47 (49.5-52-53.5-54.5)cm] from cast-on edge. BO all sts loosely.

## Finishing and Neckband

Sew in ends. Block out pieces to given dimensions.

Sew shoulder seams.

Using circular size 7 [4.5mm] needle and M/C, beg at CF with RS facing, pick up and knit 30 (31-31-33-35) sts up right front neck, knit across 34 (38-42-46-44) sts from back neck stitch holder, then pick up and knit 30 (31-31-33-35) sts down left front neck, 94 (100-104-112-114) sts. Work 4 rows in seed st. BO all sts loosely.

Sew Sleeves to body between markers placed on side seams.

Sew side and Sleeve seams.

Using crochet hook and Color D, crochet a cord 130 chains (approximately 30" [76cm] long). Thread through eyelet holes at CF opening, crossing them over each other.

Press lightly, following instructions on the yarn label.

# sun, moon, and water

A Nigerian story offers an explanation of how the earth came to be covered mostly by water.

It tells of how Sun and Moon lived together as husband and wife in a hut in Africa and had a neighbor, Water. Sun often visited Water, and one day invited her to visit him and Moon. Before Water's visit, Sun enlarged their hut in an effort to accommodate Water and all the life she contained. As Water arrived, Sun and Moon saw her grow and spread in all directions. As Water rose, Sun and Moon scrambled to the roof. Eventually their only escape was to take one giant leap up into the heavens. Moon was angry with her husband for initiating this; so she gathered up their children, the Stars, and left to live in another part of the sky. Sun misses his wife and is constantly chasing her across the skies. Moon still misses her old home on Earth, so she returns and attempts to make Water retreat from the shore.

# air

LIGHT AND BREEZY OR STRONG AND GUSTY, this element heralds changing weather patterns and brings freshness in the spring. Humans have been harnessing its transitory power for centuries, and in the form of breath, it is with us every moment of every day.

Incorporating knitting techniques that create open or lacy fabric along with the Fair Isle patterning gives the projects in this chapter lightness in feel. The denser Fair Isle sections are limited and are used at points where a more stable fabric is desirable. The silhouettes for the garments have soft lines and were chosen to feel delicate and breezy. Some projects also utilize techniques such as pleats or open cuffs, which produce gentle graceful movements during wear, further reinforcing the impression of loft. The soft, fresh-looking, pale shades of blues, purples, and grays were chosen to remind us of cloud formations. Yarns are soft, light, and gently brushed, so that they are airy to the touch.

# sway

## CARDIGAN WITH PLEATED SLEEVES

When visualizing how each element can manifest itself, a wide variety of images springs to mind—from popular culture as well as from the natural world. For example, the image of Marilyn Monroe standing over a grille holding down her skirt as a gust of air rushes up to lift her hemline has become a classic image of a sexy woman.

To give this classic cardigan some Marilyn sex appeal, pleats, which flip and sway when worn, are incorporated at the cuff—a position that maximizes their effect. The swirling Fair Isle patterns used at the front bands appear to have movement like that of gusting air currents. Rather than a sugary girly-pink, a more sophisticated shade of gray-pink is used to achieve a feminine look.

### Sizes/Finished Chest Measurements

S 34" [86cm]

M 38" [96.5cm]

L 42" [106.5cm]

XL 46" [117cm]

2X 50" [127cm]

Instructions are given for the smallest size. If changes are necessary for larger sizes, the instructions are given in ( ). Where there is only one set of figures, this applies to all sizes.

### Materials

Anti-Tickle Merino Blend DK by King Cole (100% superwash wool; 123yds [112m]/ 50g ball)

M/C, shade 280: 10 (10-12-12-13) balls

Color A, shade 162: 2 (2-2-2-2) balls

Pair each of size 6 [4mm] needles, size 7 [4.5mm] needles and size 5 [3.75mm] needles, pair of size 6 [4mm] dpns, 3 stitch holders, 5 hooks and eyes.

Yarn amounts given are based on average requirements and are approximate.

### Gauge

22 sts and 24 rows = 4" [10cm] over Fair Isle patt on size 7 [4.5mm] needles

22 sts and 28 rows = 4" [10cm] St st on size 6 [4mm] needles

Take the time to check your gauge; change the needle size if necessary to obtain the correct gauge and garment size.

REFER TO GLOSSARY ON PAGE 23 FOR: Garter Ridge

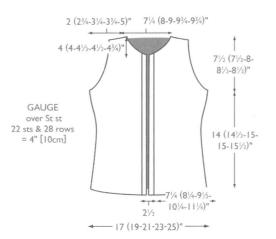

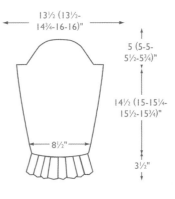

## Chart A

**Key**
- ⬜ M/C
- ⬛ A

Chart reads from L to R on WS rows, and from R to L on RS rows.

Row numbers (left): 9, 7, 5, 3, 1
Row numbers (right): 8, 6, 4, 2

— 14 st patt rep —

M | 2X ... 2X | M
L/XL S ... S L/XL
beg/end here ... beg/end here

## Chart B

**Key**
- ⬜ M/C
- ⬛ A

Chart reads from L to R on WS rows, and from R to L on RS rows.

Row numbers (left): 9, 7, 5, 3, 1
Row numbers (right): 8, 6, 4, 2

— 14 st patt rep —

M | 2X ... 2X | M
L/XL S ... S L/XL
beg/end here ... beg/end here

## Back

Using size 5 [3.75mm] needles and Color A, cast on 94 (104-116-126-138) sts. Knit 2 rows. Change to size 6 [4mm] needles and M/C, beg with a knit row, work in St st until Back measures 4¼ (4½-4½-4¾-4¾)" [11 (11.5-11.5-12-12)cm], from cast-on edge, end with RS row facing for next row.

SHAPE WAIST AS FOLLOWS:
Next row (dec row): K1, k2togb, knit to last 3 sts, k2tog, k1. Work 5 rows even.

Rep last 6 rows 3 more times, then work dec row once again, 84 (94-106-116-128) sts rem.

Work 11 rows even.

Next row (inc row): K1, m1, work to last st, m1, k1. Work 5 rows even.

Rep last 6 rows 3 more times, then work inc row once again, 94 (104-116-126-138) sts.

Work even in St st until Back measures 14 (14½-15-15-15½)" [35.5 (37-38-38-39.5)cm], end with RS row facing for next row.

SHAPE ARMHOLES AS FOLLOWS:
Cont in St st, BO 5 sts at beg of next 2 rows. Then dec 1 st at each end of next 5 rows, and 1 st at each end of following RS rows 5 times, 64 (74-86-96-108) sts rem.

Work even until armhole measures 7½ (7½-8-8½-8½)" [19 (19-20.5-21.5-21.5)cm] from beg of shaping, end with RS row facing for next row.

SHAPE SHOULDERS AS FOLLOWS:
BO 4 (5-6-7-9) sts at beg of next 6 rows. Leave rem 40 (44-50-54-54) sts on a st holder for back neck.

## Right Front

Using size 5 [3.75mm] needles and Color A, cast on 40 (46-50-56-62) sts. Knit 2 rows. Change to size 6 [4mm] needles and M/C, beg with a knit row, work in St st until Front measures 4¼ (4½-4½-4¾-4¾)" [11 (11.5-11.5-12-12)cm] from cast-on edge, end with RS row facing for next row.

SHAPE WAIST AS FOLLOWS:
Next row (dec row): Knit to last 3 sts, k2tog, k1. Work 5 rows even.

Rep last 6 rows 3 more times, then work dec row once again, 35 (41-45-51-57) sts rem.

Work 11 rows even.

Next row (inc row): Knit to last st, inc 1 st, m1, k1. Work 5 rows even.

Rep last 6 rows 3 more times, then work inc row once again, 40 (46-50-56-62) sts.

Work even in St st until Right Front measures 14 (14½-15-15-15½)" [35.5 (37-38-38-39.5)cm], end with WS row facing for next row.

SHAPE ARMHOLE AS FOLLOWS:
Cont in St st, BO 5 sts at beg of next row (this is Armhole edge). Dec 1 st at armhole edge on next 5 rows and 1 st at armhole edge on following RS rows 5 times, 25 (31-35-41-47) sts rem.

Work even until armhole measures 4½ (4½-4½-5-4¾)" [11.5 (11.5-11.5-12.5-12)cm] from beg of shaping, end with WS row facing for next row.

SHAPE FRONT NECK AS FOLLOWS:
WS row: Purl to last 5 (5-5-6-6) sts, turn (this is neck edge), slip rem sts onto a stitch holder for RH front neck.

Dec 1 st at neck edge on following 8 (11-12-14-14) rows, 12 (15-18-21-27) sts rem. Work even until Right Front measures the same as Back before shoulder shaping, end with WS row facing for next row.

SHAPE SHOULDER AS FOLLOWS:
BO 4 (5-6-7-9) sts at beg of next row. Work RS row even. Rep last 2 rows. BO rem 4 (5-6-7-9) sts.

## Left Front

Work as Right Front to beg of waist shaping, end with RS row facing for next row.

SHAPE WAIST AS FOLLOWS:
Next row (dec row): K1, k2togb, knit to end. Work 5 rows even.

Rep last 6 rows 3 more times, then work dec row once again, 35 (41-45-51-57) sts rem.

Work 11 rows even.

Next row (inc row): K1, m1, knit to end. Work 5 rows even.

Rep last 6 rows 3 more times, then work inc row once again, 40 (46-50-56-62) sts.

Work even in St st until Left Front measures 14 (14½-15-15-15½)" [35.5 (37-38-38-39)cm], end with RS row facing for next row.

SHAPE ARMHOLE AS FOLLOWS:
Cont in St st, BO 5 sts at beg of next row (this is armhole edge). Then dec 1 st at armhole edge on next 5 rows, and 1 st at armhole edge of following 5 RS rows, 25 (31-35-41-47) sts rem.

Work even until armhole measures 4½ (4½-4½-4¾-5)" [11.5 (11.5-11.5-12.5-12)cm] from beg of shaping, end with RS row facing for next row.

SHAPE FRONT NECK AS FOLLOWS:
RS row: Knit to last 5 (5-5-6-6) sts, turn (this is neck edge), slip rem sts onto a stitch holder for LH front neck.

Dec 1 st at neck edge on following 8 (11-12-14-14) rows, 12 (15-18-21-27) sts rem. Work even until Front measures the same as Back before shoulder shaping, end with RS row facing for next row.

SHAPE SHOULDER AS FOLLOWS:
BO 4 (5-6-7-9) sts at beg of next row. Work WS row even. Rep last 2 rows. BO rem 4 (5-6-7-9) sts.

## Sleeve (Make 2)

Using size 5 [3.75mm] needles and Color A, cast on 137 sts, knit 2 rows.

Change to size 6 [4mm] needles and M/C, place pleats as follows:

RS row: K10, (p1, k8, p1, k17) 4 times, 19 sts rem, p1, k8, p1, k9.

WS row: P9, (k1, p8, k1, p17) 4 times, 20 sts rem, k1, k8, k1, p10.

Rep these 2 rows until Sleeve measures 3½" [9cm] from cast-on edge, end with RS row facing for next row.

ARRANGE PLEATS AS FOLLOWS IN SUBSEQUENT DIRECTIONS:
LH Sleeve: Fold pleats so fold faces to the right by bringing RS of fabric on each dpn together. Hold both dpns together with the LH needle, placing dpns behind LH needle, as sts are knitted tog.

RH Sleeve: Fold pleats so fold faces to the left by bringing WS of fabric on each dpn together. Hold both dpns together with the LH needle, placing dpns in front of LH needle, as sts are knitted tog.

FOLD PLEATS AS FOLLOWS:
Using pair of size 6 [4mm] dpns (as well as needles already in use):

K1, *slip next 9 sts onto dpn, slip following 9 sts onto second dpn. Knit tog 1 st from each of the 3 needles/layers (arranged as described above) 9 times.

Rep from * four more times, k1, 47 sts rem.

Purl 1 row.

Change to Color A and knit 2 rows. Change back to M/C and beg with a knit row, work 4 rows in St st. Rep last 6 rows twice more.

Cont using M/C and working in St st throughout, inc 1 st at each end of next row and every following 4th row 1 (0-7-15-14) times, 51 (49-63-79-77) sts. Then inc 1 st at each end of every 6th row 12 (13-9-4-5) times, 75 (75-81-87-87) sts. Work even in St st until Sleeve measures 18 (18½-18¾-19-19¼)" [45.5 (47-47.5-48.5-49)cm] from beg.

SHAPE SLEEVE CAP FOLLOWS:
Cont in St st, BO 5 sts at beg of next 2 rows. Then dec 1 st at each end of next and following RS rows 15 (15-15-16-17) times, 33 (33-39-43-41) sts rem. BO 4 (4-6-7-6) sts at beg of next 4 rows. BO rem 17 (17-15-15-17) sts loosely.

## Left Front Band

Using size 7 [4.5mm] needles and M/C, with RS facing, pick up and knit 109 (111-113-113-121) sts down Left Front.

WS row: K3, then following Row 1 Chart A, beg at LHS of chart, work first 4 (5-6-6-3) sts as shown, then work 14 st patt rep 7 (7-7-7-8) times, 4 (5-6-6-3) sts rem, work these sts as shown at RHS of chart.

RS row: Following Row 2 Chart A, beg at RHS of chart, work first 4 (5-6-6-3) sts as shown, then work 14 st patt rep 7 (7-7-7-8) times, 7 (8-9-9-6) sts rem, work next 4 (5-6-6-3) sts as shown at LHS of chart, k3 (forms garter ridge at lower edge).

Work Rows 3–9 Chart A as set, changing colors as indicated.

RS row: Using Color A, purl 1 row (forms garter ridge).

Change to size 5 [3.75mm] needles and M/C and beg with a purl row, work 10 rows in St st. BO all sts loosely. Fold band in half at garter ridge and stitch BO edge loosely to band pickup row.

## Right Front Band

Using size 7 [4.5mm] needles and M/C, with RS facing pick up and knit 109 (111-113-113-121) sts up Right Front.

WS row: Following Row 1 Chart B, beg at LHS of chart, work first 4 (5-6-6-3) sts as shown, then work 14 st patt rep 7 (7-7-7-8) times, 7 (8-9-9-6) sts rem, work next 4 (5-6-6-3) sts as shown at RHS of chart, k3.

RS row: K3, (forms garter ridge at lower edge), then following Row 2 Chart B, beg at RHS of Chart, work first 4 (5-6-6-3) sts as shown, then work 14 st patt rep 7 (7-7-7-8) times, 4 (5-6-6-3) sts rem, work these sts as shown at LHS of chart.

Work Rows 3–9 of Chart B as set, changing colors as indicated.

RS row: Using Color A, purl 1 row (forms garter ridge).

Change to size 5 [3.75mm] needles and M/C and beg with a purl row, work 10 rows in St st. BO all sts loosely. Fold band in half at garter ridge, and stitch BO edge loosely to band pickup row.

## Neckband

Join both shoulder seams.

Using size 7 [4.5mm] needles and M/C with RS facing, pick up and knit 6 sts across top of Right Front Band (working through both layers), knit across 5 (5-5-6-6) sts from Right Front neck st holder, then pick up and knit 21 (19-23-20-27) sts up Right Front neck, knit across 40 (44-50-54-54) sts from back neck stitch holder, pick up and knit 21 (19-23-20-27) sts down Left Front neck, knit across 5 (5-5-6-6) sts from left front stitch holder, and pick up and knit 6 sts across top of Left Front Band (working through both layers), 104 (104-118-118-132) sts total.

WS row: K3, then, following Row 1 Chart A, beg at LHS of chart, work 14 st patt rep 7 (7-8-8-9) times, 3 sts rem, k3.

RS row: K3, then, following Row 2 Chart A, beg at RHS of chart, work 14 st patt rep 7 (7-8-8-9) times, 3 sts rem, k3.

Work Rows 3–9 of Chart A as set, changing colors as indicated. Using Color A, purl 1 row. Change to size 5 [3.75mm] needles and M/C, beg with a purl row, work 10 rows in St st. BO all sts loosely. Fold neckband in half at garter ridge, and stitch BO edge loosely to neckband pickup row.

## Finishing

Weave in all ends. Block all pieces to given dimensions, paying particular attention to pleats.

Set in Sleeves to Armholes. Join side and sleeve seams.

Place markers 7" [18cm] and 10" [25.5cm] down from top of neckband on Right Front Band. Place the 5 hooks at equal distances from each other between these markers, placing the top hook at highest marker and lower hook at lowest marker. Sew in place to WS of band. Sew eyes in place on WS of Left Front Band to match hooks.

Press lightly, following the instructions on the yarn label.

## harnessing wind power

Because of the power and energy that they contain, the elements have always been revered. Humans have constantly strived to invent ways to harness, contain, and convert this energy into useful forms. We understand that the power of the wind is transient. In order to make use of it, we must be flexible and inventive.

Many legends contain images of the winds being held in check by mythical beings. An Iroquois legend tells of a giant controlling the four winds, depicted in animal form, by holding their leashes. As he lessens his hold on a particular leash, that wind is allowed to blow.

# drifting

## KIDS' RAGLAN SWEATER

We closely associate the element of air with the sky. Looking upward, we daydream as we watch the clouds roll by or watch more critically to determine imminent weather changes. The speed of the clouds and the force of the wind can give us clues to these changes.

Cloud formations inspired me to create this pattern. Selected for their rounded, cloudlike shapes, the motifs used in the Fair Isle section for this project are not symmetrical, but rather offset to give a hint of movement like drifting clouds. The several variations of blues and mauves evoke a moody feeling just as shifting weather patterns do when they transform the sky.

## Sizes/Finished Chest Measurements

12 months 23" [58.5cm]

18 months 25½" [65cm]

2 years 27½" [70cm]

3 years 30" [76cm]

Instructions are given for the smallest size. If changes are necessary for larger sizes, the instructions are given in ( ). Where there is only one set of figures, this applies to all sizes.

## Materials

Anti-Tickle Merino Blend DK by King Cole (100% superwash wool; 123yds [112m]/50g ball)

*green*
*12 rose*
Color A, shade 47: 2 (3-3-3) balls

Color B, shade 174: 1 ball *Navy blue*

*DK grn* Color C, shade 18: 1 ball

Color D, shade 94: 1 ball *Wine purple*

Color E, 175: 1 ball *gold*

Color F, shade 13: 2 balls *Lt Blue*

Pair each of size 6 [4mm] and size 7 [4.5mm] needles, 4 stitch holders, 8 buttons

Yarn amounts given are based on average requirements and are approximate.

## Gauge

26 sts and 24 rows = 4" [10cm] over Fair Isle patt on size 7 [4.5mm] needles.

22 sts and 28 rows = 4" [10cm] over St st on size 6 [4mm] needles.

Take the time to check your gauge; change the needle size if necessary to obtain the correct gauge and garment size.

REFER TO GLOSSARY ON PAGE 23 FOR: Garter Ridges, Seed Stitch

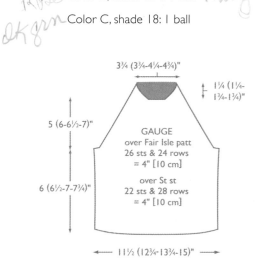

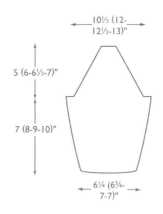

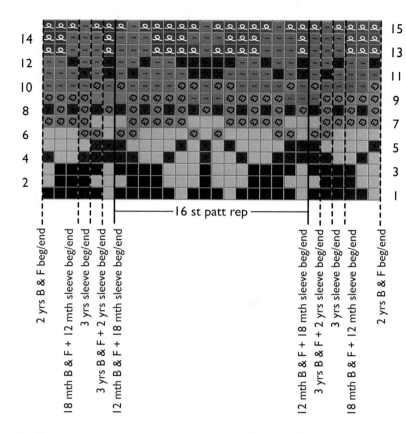

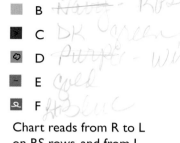

**Key**

| | | |
|---|---|---|
| ■ | A | green |
| ▨ | B | ~~Hoy~~ Rose |
| ▸ | C | DK green |
| ◔ | D | Purple - Wine |
| ~ | E | Gold |
| ℗ | F | Blue |

Chart reads from R to L
on RS rows, and from L
to R on WS rows.

Chart labels (left to right): 2 yrs B & F beg/end · 18 mth B & F + 12 mth sleeve beg/end · 3 yrs sleeve beg/end · 3 yrs B & F + 2 yrs sleeve beg/end · 12 mth B & F + 18 mth sleeve beg/end · —16 st patt rep— · 12 mth B & F + 18 mth sleeve beg/end · 3 yrs B & F + 2 yrs sleeve beg/end · 3 yrs sleeve beg/end · 18 mth B & F + 12 mth sleeve beg/end · 2 yrs B & F beg/end

## Back

Using size 6 [4mm] needles and Color A, cast on 59 (65-71-77) sts. Work 2 rows in seed st. Purl 1 row.

Eyelet row: K1, *YO, k2tog; rep from * to end.

Change to Color D, knit 2 rows. Change to Color B, knit 2 rows (forms garter ridges).

Using Color A, knit 1 row, inc 5 sts evenly across row, 64 (70-76-82) sts.

Beg with a purl row, work in St st until Back measures 3½ (4-4½-5¼)" [9 (10-11.5-13)cm], end with RS row facing for next row. 2y Ruffle

Change to size 7 [4.5mm] needles.

PLACE FAIR ISLE PATT AS FOLLOWS:
RS row: Following Row 1 of chart, beg at RHS of chart, work first 0 (3-6-1) sts as shown, then work 16 st patt rep 4 (4-4-5) times, 0 (3-6-1) sts rem, work these as shown at LHS of chart.

WS row: Following Row 2 of chart, beg at LHS, work first 0 (3-6-1) sts as shown, then work 16 st patt rep 4 (4-

4-5) times, 0 (3-6-1) sts rem, work as shown at RHS of chart.

Fair Isle patt is now set, work Rows 3–15 in sequence as set, changing colors as indicated.

Change to size 6 [4mm] needles and Color F, purl 1 row.

SHAPE RAGLANS AS FOLLOWS:
Working in St st throughout, beg with a knit row, BO 5 (5-5-6) sts at beg of next 2 rows. Then dec 1 st at each end of next 17 (20-21-23) RS rows. Place rem 20 (20-24-26) sts on a stitch holder for back neck.

## Front

Work as given for Back until 30 (30-38-40) sts rem during raglan shaping, end with RS row facing for next row.

SHAPE FRONT NECK AS FOLLOWS:
RS row: Cont in St st, dec 1 st at beg of row, work until there are 12 (12-15-15) sts on needle, turn (this is neck edge). Leave rem 17 (17-22-24) sts on a spare needle.

Working on the 12 (12-15-15) sts only, dec 1 st at neck edge on the next 4 (4-2-2) rows, *at the same time*

dec 1 st at raglan edge on RS rows only, 6 (6-12-12) sts rem. Cont dec at raglan edge as before (every RS row), dec 1 st at neck edge on following 2 (2-5-5) RS rows, 2 sts rem, k2tog, break off yarn and draw through loop.

Return to sts on spare needle, slip center 4 (4-6-8) sts onto a stitch holder and rejoin Color F, knit to end, dec 1 st at end of row, 12 (12-15-15) sts rem.

Dec 1 st at neck edge on the next 4 (4-2-2) rows, *at the same time* dec 1 st at raglan edge on RS rows only, 6 (6-12-12) sts rem. Cont dec at raglan edge as before (every RS row), dec 1 st at neck edge on following 2 (2-5-5) RS rows, 2 sts rem, k2tog, break off yarn and draw through loop.

## Sleeve (Make 2)

Using size 6 [4mm] needles and Color A, cast on 35 (37-39-39) sts, work 2 rows in seed st. Purl 1 row. Work eyelet row and garter ridges as given for Back.

Change to Color A, knit 1 row, inc 5 sts evenly across row, 40 (42-44-44) sts.

Beg with a purl row, work in St st, *at the same time* inc 1 st at each end of row 3 and every following 2nd row 1 (5-1-0) times, 44 (54-48-46). Then inc 1 st at each end of every following 4th row 5 (5-9-11) times, 54 (64-66-68) sts.

Change to size 7 [4.5mm] needles.

### PLACE FAIR ISLE PATT AS FOLLOWS:

RS row: Following Row 1 of chart, work first 3 (0-1-2) sts as shown at RHS of chart, then work 16 st patt rep 3 (4-4-4) times, 3 (0-1-2) sts rem, work as shown at LHS of chart.

WS row: Following Row 2 of chart, work first 3 (0-1-2) sts as shown at LHS of chart, then work 16 st patt rep 3 (4-4-4) times, 3 (0-1-2) sts rem, work as shown at RHS of chart.

Fair Isle patt is now set, work Rows 3–15 in sequence as set, changing colors as indicated, *at the same time* inc 1 st at each end of Rows 5 and 11, 58 (68-70-72) sts, work inc sts in patt as appropriate.

Change back to size 6 [4mm] needles and Color F, work even until Sleeve measures 7 (8-9-10)" [18 (20-23-25.5)cm] from beg, end with RS row facing for next row.

### SHAPE RAGLAN AS FOLLOWS:

Working in St st throughout, beg with a knit row, BO 5 sts at beg of next 2 rows. Then dec 1 st at each end of every RS row 14 (17-18-19) times, 20 (24-24-24) sts rem. Then dec 1 st at each end of every row 6 (8-8-8) times, 8 sts rem. Leave these sts on a stitch holder.

## Finishing and Neckband

Block all pieces to given dimensions. Join both back raglan seams. Join BO sections at beg of raglan shaping for front raglan seams. Leave the rest of front raglan seams open.

### WORK FRONT RAGLAN OPENINGS AS FOLLOWS:

With RS facing, using size 6 [4mm] needles and Color F, pick up and knit 38 (40-42-46) sts along right sleeve raglan edge. Work 3 rows in seed st. BO all sts in patt.

Rep for left sleeve raglan edge.

Rep for right front raglan edge.

With RS facing, using size 6 [4mm] needles and Color F, pick up and knit 38 (40-42-46) sts along left front raglan edge. Work 1 row in seed st, RS row facing for next row.

### WORK BUTTONHOLE ROW AS FOLLOWS:

Work 0 (0-0-4) sts in seed st, *work 8 sts in seed st, k2tog, (YO) twice, k2tog; rep from * twice more, work rem 2 (4-6-6) sts in seed st.

Work 1 row in seed st, working 2 sts in each double YO. BO all sts in patt.

### WORK BACK NECKBAND AS FOLLOWS:

With RS facing, using size 6 [4mm] needles and Color F, beg at right raglan sleeve edge, pick up and knit 4 sts across band, knit across 8 sts from right sleeve stitch holder, knit across 20 (20-24-26) sts from back neck st holder, knit across 8 sts from left sleeve, then pick up and knit 4 sts across left raglan edge band, 44 (44-48-50) sts total. Work 1 row in seed st.

### WORK EYELET ROW AS FOLLOWS:

K1, *YO, k2tog; rep from * to last st, k1.

Work 2 rows in seed st working 2 sts into double YO. BO all sts in patt.

### WORK FRONT NECKBAND AS FOLLOWS:

With RS facing, using size 6 [4mm] needles and Color F, beg at left front raglan edge, pick up and knit 18 (18-20-22) sts across band and down left front neck, knit 4 (4-6-8) sts from front neck stitch holder, then pick up and knit 18 (18-20-22) sts up right front neck and raglan edge band, 40 (40-46-52) sts total.

Work 1 row in seed st.

### WORK EYELET AND BUTTONHOLE ROW AS FOLLOWS:

K2, k2tog, (YO) twice, k2tog, *YO, k2tog; rep from * to last 2 sts, k2.

Work 2 rows in seed st, working 2 sts into double YO. BO all sts in patt.

Join side and sleeve seams.

Sew on buttons to correspond to buttonholes on LHS and through both layers at same points on RHS.

Press lightly, following the instructions on the yarn label.

# winged creatures

In storybooks that we might remember from childhood, nature's elements are depicted as creatures from beyond our world, such as fairies, gnomes, nymphs, and elves. Some of them use plant material to make their homes, live underground or underwater, and many can fly. They use their wings to drop into our world and disappear without being seen or heard. The longevity of these stories and the ability of these fantasy creatures to capture our imagination are probably reflections of our secret desire to possess these powers. . . . Or maybe we just want to get away with mischievous acts.

# breeze

## WOMEN'S CAP SLEEVE TOP

The fresh winds of spring blow away the doldrums of the winter months, clearing the way for more carefree lazy days. This change heralds a desire for cleansing and transition in our wardrobe. Suddenly we long to feel soft breezes on our skin, so we choose more liberating garments with open necklines and shorter sleeves.

An unusual fretted openwork stitch, formed by crossing elongated stitches over each other, is incorporated into this project to lighten the weight of the fabric. Soft sky blues predominate, with a warmer shade of pale coral defining the delicate Fair Isle patterned border. The openwork stitch is repeated to trim the sleeves and the simple open V-neck.

### Sizes/Finished Chest Measurements

S 32.5" [82.5cm]

M 37" [94cm]

L 41½" [105cm]

XL 43½" [110.5cm]

2X 48" [122cm]

3X 52" [132cm]

Instructions are given for the smallest size. If changes are necessary for larger sizes, the instructions are given in ( ). Where there is only one set of figures, this applies to all sizes.

### Materials

Basics—Stop by Lana Grossa (50% viscose, 50% microfiber; 115yds [105m]/50g ball)

M/C, shade 12: 8 (8-9-10-11-13) balls

Color A, shade 04: 1 (1-1-2-2-2) ball

Color B, shade 07: 1 ball

Pair each of size 6 [4mm] and size 7 [4.5mm] needles, size 7 [4.5mm] circular needle (16" [40cm] long) for neckband, stitch holder.

Yarn amounts given are based on average requirements and are approximate.

### Gauge

22 sts and 24 rows = 4" [10cm] over Fair Isle patt on size 7 [4.5mm] needles.

22 sts and 30 rows = 4" [10cm] over St st on size 6 [4mm] needles.

Take the time to check your gauge; change the needle size if necessary to obtain the correct gauge and garment size.

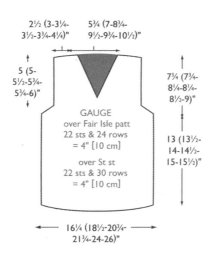

2½ (3-3¼-3½-3¾-4¼)"    5¾ (7-8¾-9½-9¾-10½)"

5 (5-5½-5¾-5¾-6)"

GAUGE
over Fair Isle patt
22 sts & 24 rows
= 4" [10 cm]

over St st
22 sts & 30 rows
= 4" [10 cm]

7¾ (7¾-8¼-8¼-8½-9)"

13 (13½-14-14½-15-15½)"

16¼ (18½-20¾-21¾-24-26)"

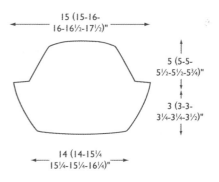

15 (15-16-16-16½-17½)"

5 (5-5-5½-5½-5¾)"

3 (3-3-3¼-3¼-3½)"

14 (14-15¼-15¼-15¼-16¼)"

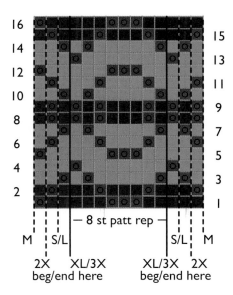

16
15
14
13
12
11
10
9
8
7
6
5
4
3
2
1

— 8 st patt rep —

M | S/L | S/L | M

2X
XL/3X
beg/end here
XL/3X
2X
beg/end here

**Key**

■ M/C

■ A

◉ B

Chart reads from R to L
on RS rows, and from L
to R on WS rows.

## Openwork Pattern (6 St Patt Rep)

Row 1 (RS): Knit.

Row 2: K3, *(Knit next st wrapping yarn around needle twice) rep from * to last 3 sts, k3.

Row 3: K3, *slip next 6 sts onto RH needle dropping extra wraps, keeping all sts in their correct order, pass first set of 3 sts over second set of 3 sts letting them drop off needle, pass rem 3 sts back onto LH needle and knit into the front and back of each of them; rep from * to last 3 sts, k3.

Rep Rows 1–3 for patt, note that on second rep, RS rows are now WS rows and vice versa.

## Back

Using size 7 [4.5mm] needles and M/C, cast on 90 (102-114-120-132-144) sts. Knit 1 row.

Work in Openwork Patt for 9 rows (3 reps of patt). Place markers at each end of last row.

### PLACE FAIR ISLE BORDER AS FOLLOWS:
RS row: Following Row 1 of chart, beg at RHS of chart, work first 1 (3-1-0-2-0) sts as shown, then work 8 st patt rep 11 (12-14-15-16-18) times, 1 (3-1-0-2-0) sts rem, work these as shown at LHS of chart.

WS row: Following Row 2 of chart, beg at LHS of chart, work first 1 (3-1-0-2-0) sts as shown, then work 8 st patt rep 11 (12-14-15-16-18) times, 1 (3-1-0-2-0) sts rem, work these as shown at RHS of chart.

Work Rows 3–16 of chart in sequence as set, changing colors as indicated.

Change to size 6 [4mm] needles and beg with a knit row, work in St st until Back measures 13 (13½-14-14½-15-15½)" [33 (34.5-35.5-37-38-39.5)cm] from cast-on edge, end with RS row facing for next row.

### SHAPE ARMHOLES AS FOLLOWS:
Cont in St st, BO 5 (5-5-5-6-7) sts at beg of next 2 rows. Then dec 1 st at each end of next 5 (5-5-5-7-7) rows and 1 st at each end of following RS rows 5 times, 60 (72-84-90-96-106) sts rem.

Work even until armhole measures 7¾ (7¾-8¼-8¼-8½-9)" [19.5 (19.5-21-21-21.5-23)cm] from beg of shaping, end with RS row facing for next row.

### SHAPE SHOULDERS AS FOLLOWS:
BO 5 (6-6-6-7-8) sts at beg of next 4 rows. Then BO 4 (5-6-7-7-8) sts at beg of next 2 rows. Leave rem 32 (38-48-52-54-58) sts on a st holder for back neck.

## Front

Work as given for Back until armhole shaping is complete. Purl 1 row.

### DIVIDE FOR V-NECK AND WORK LHS AS FOLLOWS:
RS row: K30 (36-42-45-48-53), turn (this is neck edge), leave rem 30 (36-42-45-48-53) sts on a spare needle for RH front.

Dec 1 st at neck edge on next 0 (0-6-8-12-12) rows. Then dec 1 st at neck edge on each RS row 14 (18-18-18-15-17) times. Then dec 1 st at neck edge on every 4th row 2 (1-0-0-0-0) times. 14 (17-18-19-21-24) sts rem.

Work even until Front measures the same as Back before shoulder shaping, end with RS row facing for next row.

### SHAPE SHOULDER AS FOLLOWS:
BO 5 (6-6-6-7-8) sts at beg of next row. Work WS row even. Rep last 2 rows. BO rem 4 (5-6-7-7-8) sts.

### WORK RHS AS FOLLOWS:
Return to sts on spare needle, rejoin M/C, and knit to end.

Dec 1 st at neck edge on next 0 (0-6-8-12-12) rows. Then dec 1 st at neck edge on each RS row 14 (18-18-18-15-17) times. Then dec 1 st at neck edge on every 4th row 2 (1-0-0-0-0) times, 14 (17-18-19-21-24) sts rem.

Work even until Front measures the same as Back before shoulder shaping, end with WS row facing for next row.

### SHAPE SHOULDER AS FOLLOWS:
BO 5 (6-6-6-7-8) sts at beg of next row. Work RS row even. Rep last 2 rows. BO rem 4 (5-6-7-7-8) sts.

## Sleeve (Make 2)

Using size 7 [4.5mm] needles and M/C, cast on 78 (78-84-84-84-90) sts, knit 1 row.

Work Rows 1–3 given for Openwork Patt.

Change to size 6 [4mm] needles, beg with a purl row, work in St st throughout, *at the same time* inc 1 st at each end of row 4 and every following 6th row 1 (1-1-1-2-2) time, 82 (82-88-88-90-96) sts. Work even until Sleeve measures 3 (3-3-3¼-3¼-3½)" [7.5 (7.5-7.5-8-8-9)cm] from cast-on edge, ending with a RS row facing for next row.

SHAPE SLEEVE CAP FOLLOWS:
Cont in St st BO 5 (5-5-5-6-7) sts at beg of next 2 rows. Then dec 1 st at each end of next row and following RS rows 16 (16-16-18-18-19) times, 38 (38-44-40-40-42) sts rem. BO 6 (6-7-6-6-6) sts at beg of next 4 rows. BO rem 14 (14-16-16-16-18) sts loosely.

## Finishing and Neckband

Weave in all ends. Block pieces to given dimensions.

Join both shoulder seams.

Using circular size 7 [4.5mm] needle and M/C, beg at CF V-neck divide with RS facing, pick up and knit 44 (44-48-49-51-52) sts up right front neck, knit across 32 (38-48-52-54-58) sts from back neck stitch holder, then pick up and knit 44 (44-48-49-51-52) sts down left front neck, 120 (126-144-150-156-162) sts total. Work Rows 2 (WS) and 3 in Openwork Patt. Knit 1 row. BO all sts knitwise.

Allow neckband to cross over at CF and stitch in place.

Set Sleeves into armholes. Join Sleeve and side seams, leaving side seams open at lower edges below markers.

Press lightly, following the instructions on the yarn label.

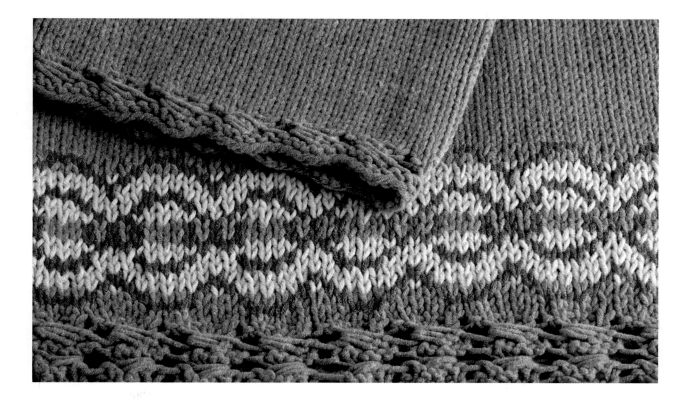

Proudly proclaiming its presence, a flag fluttering on a rooftop catches the eye and draws our attention. Using a piece of cloth to catch the wind is a very simple ritual, but one that is practiced by many cultures. It is used for celebration, to pledge allegiance, as protest, and even as a prayer offering.

   Small colorful Tibetan prayer flags are called wind-horses. Their origin is militaristic—once used to call for a massing of the clans. Now, they are adorned with symbols, mantras, and prayers and are raised on auspicious days. As the flags flap, it is believed that the prayers are carried by the wind to the deities. Their colors represent the five Tibetan elements of earth, water, fire, wind, and space.

# swirl

## LACY WRAP WITH FAIR ISLE BORDERS

All the elements have associated motions—from calm to raging. Air can manifest itself as a gentle breeze off the ocean or as a fierce tornado. It can also be subtle and furtive, finding openings to creep through, its icy touch making us chilled and uncomfortable.

This wrap feels as light as air, and it is designed to keep out unwelcome breezes by enveloping the neckline and shoulders. Its barely-there feel makes it suitable for air-conditioned rooms during the summer months or as an extra layer of cozy warmth over a jacket in the winter. Its Fair Isle bands and oversized lacy pattern add drama and sophistication to a simple construction.

### Finished Measurements

Wrap measures 82" [208cm] long and 17" [43cm] wide.

### Materials

La Gran by Classic Elite (76.5% mohair, 17.5% wool, 6% nylon; 90yds [82m]/42g ball)

M/C, Crepe Myrtle shade 6589: 5 balls

Color A, Eucalyptus Green shade 6539: 1 ball

Color B, Pebble shade 6575: 1 ball

Size 11 [8mm] circular needle, size K/10½ [6.5mm] crochet hook

Yarn amounts given are based on average requirements and are approximate.

### Gauge

14 sts and 15 rows = 4" [10cm] over Fair Isle patt on size 11 [8mm] needles

10.5 sts and 15 rows = 4" [10cm] over Lace patt on size 11 [8mm] needles

Take the time to check your gauge; change the needle size if necessary to obtain the correct gauge and garment size.

REFER TO TECHNIQUES ON PAGE 18 FOR: Single Crochet

### Special Abbreviation

double dec: slip 2 stitches together knitwise, knit 1, pass both slipped stitches over.

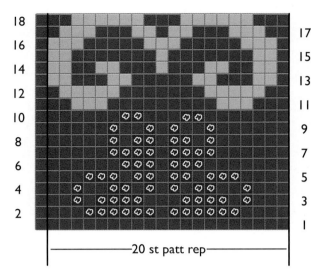

**Key**

🗘 M/C

⬛ A

🔲 B

Chart reads from R to L on RS rows,
and from L to R on WS rows.

─20 st patt rep─

## Lace Pattern
### (16 St Patt Rep Plus 17 Sts)

Row 1: Knit.

Row 2: Purl.

Row 3: (K1, YO) 3 times, * (sl 1, k1, psso) twice, work double dec, (k2tog) twice, (YO, k1) 5 times, YO, rep from * to last 14 sts, (sl 1, k1, psso) twice, work double dec, (k2tog) twice, (YO, k1) 3 times.

Row 4: Purl.

Rows 5–16: Rep Rows 1–4 three times.

Row 17: Knit.

Row 18: Purl.

Row 19: (K2tog) 3 times, *(YO, k1) 5 times, YO, (sl 1, k1, psso) twice, work double dec, (k2tog) twice, rep from * to last 11 sts, (YO, k1) 5 times, YO, (sl 1, k1, psso) 3 times.

Row 20: Purl.

Rows 21–32: Rep Rows 17–20 three times.

Rep Rows 1–32 for patt.

Using size 11 [8mm] circular needle and M/C, cast on 193 sts using the knitted-on method to produce a loose edge.

Working back and forth in rows, work in Lace Pattern, rep Rows 1–32 of patt twice.

BO as follows:

P2, *slip these sts back onto LH needle, p2tog (the 2 sts just slipped onto LH needle), 1 st now on RH needle, p1; rep from * to end.

WORK LOWER EDGE BORDERS AS
FOLLOWS:
**Using size 11 (8 mm) needle and Color A, with RS facing, pick up and knit 61 sts across one short end of wrap. Purl 1 row.

RS row: Following Row 1 of chart, beg at RHS of chart work 20 st patt rep 3 times, 1 st rem, work this st as shown at LHS of chart.

WS row: Following Row 2 of chart, beg at LHS of chart, work first st as shown, then work 20 st patt rep 3 times.

Work Rows 3–18 of chart as set, changing colors as indicated.

USING M/C, WORK EYELET ROW
AS FOLLOWS:
K1, *YO, k2tog; rep from * to end.

Beg with a purl row, work 3 rows in St st.

Change to Color B and work another 14 rows in St st. BO all sts very loosely.

Rep from ** for second border across other short end of wrap.

Sew in all ends. Block wrap to given dimensions, ensuring that the Lace Patt waves along long edges of wrap.

Fold lower edge border facings along eyelet rows and stitch to pick-up row of each border.

Using M/C and crochet hook, work a single crochet edge along each side edge of lower borders, working through both layers.

Press lightly, following the instructions on the yarn label

## aeolos, greek ruler of the winds

In Greek mythology, the predominant characters tend to be gods and goddesses. They appear to come from complicted lineages, but when viewed in terms of the natural world many of these relationships follow logical paths. Aeolos, who ruled the winds and is credited with inventing sails, was the son of Poseidon, god of the sea. He was married to Eos, goddess of the dawn, who bore the children Zephyr, Boreas, Eurus, and Notos—the winds of the West, North, East, and South. Because of Aeolos's close links to both sea and wind, he appears in the stories of heroes on epic voyages. One such legend tells of Odysseus traveling across the oceans after his success at Troy. Aeolos gives him a leather bag containing all the contrary winds for his journey. All goes well until his crew, believing that he has gold hidden in the bag, opens it releasing all the winds, which are now free to hinder his progress.

# whisper

## TURTLENECK WITH LACE AND FAIR ISLE ACCENTS

Air is the opposite of earth both physically and emotionally. The delicacy and lightness of anything described as airy is in marked contrast to the grounded practical feeling associated with earthbound things, and each extreme evokes a different response from us. Imagine the gracefulness of a soaring ballerina contrasted with the steady rhythm of a military march, or the thought of a lightly whipped dessert compared to a wholesome stick-to-the-ribs bread pudding.

Lightweight and lofty, the yarn used for this sweater gives it a wispy feel. Using lace patterning for the cuffs and collar opens up the fabric to further achieve this effect. The Fair Isle pattern, producing a denser fabric, is used at the shoulders for stability and on the sleeve like a tiny jeweled bracelet.

### Sizes/Finished Chest Measurements

XS 35" [89cm]

S 39" [99cm]

M 42" [106.5cm]

L 46" [117cm]

XL 50" [127cm]

2X 54" [137cm]

Instructions are given for the smallest size. If changes are necessary for larger sizes, the instructions are given in ( ). If there is only one set of figures, this applies to all sizes.

### Materials

Angorissima by Diamond Yarn (100% angora; 123yds [114 m]/25 g ball)

M/C, shade 1504: 10 (10-11-12-14-15) balls

Color A, shade 1017: 1 (1-1-1-2-2) balls

Color B, shade 099: 1 (1-1-2-2-2) balls

Pair of size 7 [4.5mm] needles, size 7 [4.5mm] circular needle (16" [40.5cm] long) for turtleneck, size 8 [5mm] circular needle for BO, size G/6 [4mm] crochet hook for neatening sleeve seams, 6 stitch holders

Yarn amounts given are based on average requirements and are approximate.

### Gauge

24 sts and 28 rows = 4" [10cm] over St st on size 7 [4.5mm] needles.

Take the time to check your gauge; change the needle size if necessary to obtain the correct gauge and garment size.

REFER TO TECHNIQUES ON PAGE 18 FOR: Short Rows, Single Crochet, 3-Needle Bind-Off

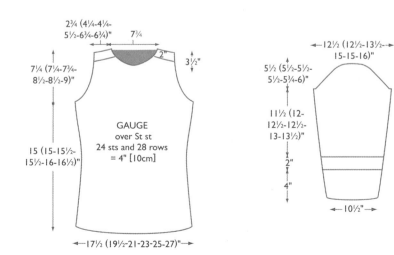

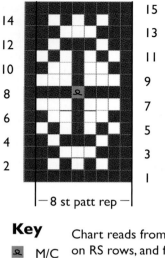

— 8 st patt rep —

**Key**

⚬ M/C   Chart reads from R to L on RS rows, and from L to R on WS rows.

■ A

□ B

## Lace Pattern
### (6 St Patt Rep, Plus 3 Sts)

Row 1 (RS): K2, *YO, ssk, k1, k2tog, YO, k1; rep from * to last st, k1.

Rows 2, 4, 6, and 8: Purl all sts when working cuff, knit all sts when working turtleneck.

Row 3: K2, *YO, k1, sl1-k2tog-psso, k1, YO, k1; rep from * to last st, k1.

Row 5: K2, *k2tog, YO, k1, YO, ssk, k1; rep from * to last st, k1.

Row 7: K1, k2tog, *(k1, YO) twice, k1, sl1-k2tog-psso; rep from * to last 6 sts, (k1, YO) twice, k1, ssk, k1.

Rep Rows 1–8 for patt.

## Back

Using size 7 [4.5mm] needles and M/C, cast on 105 (117-125-137-149-161) sts. Knit 2 rows. Then, beg with a knit row, work in St st until Back measures 3¾ (3¾-4-4-4-4½)" [9.5 (9.5-10-10-10-11.5)cm] from beg, end with RS row facing for next row.

SHAPE WAIST AS FOLLOWS:
Dec 1 st at each end of next row. Work 3 rows even. Rep last 4 rows 4 more times, plus dec row once again, 93 (105-113-125-137-149) sts rem.

Work 9 rows even.

Inc 1 st at each end of next row. Work 3 rows even. Rep last 4 rows 4 more times, plus inc row once again, 105 (117-125-137-149-161) sts.

Work even until Back measures 15 (15-15½-15½-16-16½)" [38 (38-39.5-39.5-40.5-42)cm] from beg, end with RS row facing for next row.

SHAPE ARMHOLES AS FOLLOWS:
BO 4 sts at beg of next 2 rows and 3 sts at beg of following 2 rows, 91 (103-111-123-135-147) sts. Dec 1 st at each end of next 4 rows, then dec 1 st at each end of following 4 (2-4-4-2-6) RS rows, 75 (91-95-107-123-127) sts.

Work even until armhole measures 5¼ (5¼-5¾-6½-6½-7)" [13.5 (13.5-14.5-16.5-16.5-18)cm], from beg of shaping, end with WS row facing for next row.

SHAPE SHOULDERS, WORKING IN SHORT ROWS, AS FOLLOWS (NOTE THIS OCCURS LOWER THAN USUAL):
Next 2 rows: Work to last 6 (8-8-11-14-14) sts, wrap next st, turn.

Next 2 rows: Work to last 12 (16-16-22-28-28) sts, wrap next st, turn.

Next 2 rows: Work to last 17 (25-25-33-41-41) sts, wrap next st, turn.

Work across WS row, working the wraps tog with the st they wrap.

Work across RS row, working the wraps tog with the st they wrap.

Next WS row: Purl, inc 6 (6-2-6-6-2) sts evenly across row, 81 (97-97-113-129-129) sts.

PLACE FAIR ISLE PATT AS FOLLOWS:
RS row: Following Row 1 of chart, beg at RHS, work 8 st patt rep 10 (12-12-14-16-16) times across row, 1 st rem, work as shown at LHS of chart.

WS row: Following Row 2 of chart, beg at LHS, work first st as shown, then work 8 st patt rep 10 (12-12-14-16-16) times.

Fair Isle patt is now set. Cont rep Rows 3–15 of chart:

Place 17 (25-25-33-41-41) sts on a stitch holder for RH shoulder, the center 47 sts on a second st holder for back neck, and rem 17 (25-25-33-41-41) sts on a third stitch holder for LH shoulder.

## Front

Work as given for Back until armhole shaping is complete, 75 (91-95-107-123-127) sts.

Work even until armhole measures 4¼ (4¼-4¾-5½-5½-6)" [11 (11-12-14-14-15)cm], end with RS row facing for next row.

SHAPE FRONT NECK AS FOLLOWS:
Work across 28 (36-36-44-52-52) sts, turn (this is neck edge). Leave rem 47 (55-59-63-71-75) sts on a st holder. Working on the 28 (36-36-44-52-52) sts only, and working all RS rows even thoroughout, BO 4 sts at beg of next row, then BO 3 sts at beg of following WS rows twice, then dec 1 st at beg of following WS row, 17 (25-25-33-41-41) sts rem. Work RS row even.

SHAPE LEFT SHOULDER AS FOLLOWS:
WS row: Work to last 6 (8-8-11-14-14) sts, wrap next st, turn.

Work RS row even.

Next WS row: Work to last 12 (16-16-22-28-28) sts, wrap next st, turn.

Work RS row even.

Next WS row: Work across all sts working wrap tog with the st it wraps.

PLACE FAIR ISLE PATT AS FOLLOWS:
RS row: Following Row 1 of chart, beg at RHS, work the 8 st patt rep 2 (3-3-4-5-5) times across row, 1 st rem, work as shown at LHS of chart.

WS row: Following Row 2 of chart, beg at LHS, work first st as shown, then work 8 st patt rep 2 (3-3-4-5-5) times.

Fair Isle patt is now set. Work Rows 3–15, changing colors as indicated.

Leave these sts on a st holder for shoulder seam.

Return to sts on spare needle. Slip center 19 (19-23-19-19-23) sts onto a st holder for front neck. Rejoin yarn to rem 28 (36-36-44-52-52) sts. Working all WS rows even thoroughout, BO 4 sts at beg of row, then BO 3 sts at beg of following RS row twice, then dec 1 st at beg of following RS row, 17 (25-

25-33-41-41) sts rem. Work WS row even.

### SHAPE RIGHT SHOULDER AS FOLLOWS:

RS row: Work to last 6 (8-8-11-14-14) sts, wrap next st, turn.

Work WS row even.

Next RS row: Work to last 12 (16-16-22-28-28) sts, wrap next st, turn.

Work WS row even.

Next RS row: Work across all sts, working wraps tog with the st they wrap.

Work WS row even.

### PLACE FAIR ISLE PATT AS FOLLOWS:

RS row: Following Row 1 of chart, beg at RHS, work 8 st patt rep 2 (3-3-4-5-5) times across row, 1 st rem, work as shown at LHS of chart.

WS row: Following Row 2 of chart, beg at LHS, work first st as shown, then work 8 st patt rep 2 (3-3-4-5-5) times.

Fair Isle patt is now set. Work Rows 3–15, changing colors as indicated.

Leave these sts on a st holder for shoulder seam.

## Sleeve (Make 2)

Using size 7 [4.5mm] needles and M/C, cast on 63 sts. Knit 2 rows. Work in Lace Patt (purling all even-numbered rows) until Sleeve measures 4" [10cm] from beg, end with RS row facing for next row, inc 1 st at each end of last WS row, 65 sts.

### PLACE FAIR ISLE PATT AS FOLLOWS:

RS row: Following Row 1 of chart, beg at RHS, work 8 st patt rep 8 times across row, 1 st rem, work as shown at LHS of chart.

WS row: Following Row 2 of chart, beg at LHS, work first st as shown, then work 8 st patt rep 8 times.

Fair Isle patt is now set. Work Rows 3–15, changing colors as indicated.

Using M/C, beg with a purl row, work in St st throughout *at the same time* inc 1 st at each end of next row and every following 16 (16-10-8-8-6)th row 4 (4-4-5-6-15) times, 75 (75-75-77-79-97) sts. Then inc 1 st at each end of every 0 (0-12-6-6-0)th row 0 (0-3-7-6-0) times, 75 (75-81-91-91-97) sts.

Work even until Sleeve measures 17½ (18-18½-18½-19-19½)" [44.5 (45.5-47-47-48-49.5)cm], from cast-on edge, end with RS row facing for next row.

### SHAPE SLEEVE CAP AS FOLLOWS:

Cont in St st, BO 4 sts at beg of next 2 rows, then 3 sts at beg of following 2 rows. Dec 1 st at each end of every following RS row 15 (15-15-15-16-17) times, 31 (31-37-47-45-49) sts rem. BO 3 (3-4-6-6-7) sts at beg of next 4 rows. BO rem 19 (19-21-23-21-21) sts using size 8 [5mm] needle.

## Finishing and Turtleneck

Weave in all ends. Block all pieces to given dimensions.

Join both shoulder seams using the 3-needle bind-off method.

Using circular size 7 [4.5mm] needle and M/C, with RS facing and beg at LH shoulder seam, pick up and knit 29 (29-30-32-35-36) sts down left front neck, knit across 19 (19-23-19-19-23) sts from front neck st holder, then pick up and knit 28 (28-29-31-34-35) sts up right front neck, knit across 47 sts from back neck st holder, 123 (123-129-129-135-141) sts total.

Place marker to indicate beg of rnd. Knit 20 rnds, on last rnd work 1 st beyond marker, wrap next st, turn to reverse direction of work (WS of garment is now facing). Beg with Row 1 of patt, work in Lace Patt until Turtleneck measures 6" [15cm] from pickup row (knitting all even-numbered rows).

Next rnd: Knit into front and back of each st, 246 (246-258-258-270-282) sts.

BO all sts loosely using size 8 [5mm] needle.

Set in Sleeves to armholes. Sew side and Sleeve seams, leaving lower 4" [10cm] of sleeve seam open. Using crochet hook and M/C, work in single crochet along openings in Sleeve seams. Turn turtleneck down so that the RS of Lace Patt is facing.

Press lightly, following the instructions on the yarn label.

## mauve

We take for granted the wide diversity of textile colors available to us. Before the invention of synthetic dyes, the color palette for clothing was severely limited. Even though dyes came from natural sources, the extraction process could be lengthy and availability limited. So the discovery of the first synthetic dye by William Perkin in the 1850s heralded an expansion in color availability.

The discovery, as in all the best stories, was completely accidental. Perkin was trying to synthesize an artificial equivalent for quinine to treat malaria. But what he produced was a substance that could dye silk a beautiful shade of mauve.

# fire

FROM THE BRIGHTNESS OF THE SUN'S RAYS to the warmth of a fireside, from the destructive power of a raging inferno to the flame's ability to purify, this element is associated with both festivity and sadness. Its heat can be either welcome or disagreeable.

The color palette for this chapter was easy to choose—bright, warm tones of reds, oranges, and yellows. These colors instantly make us feel cheerful and cozy. But just like fire, they need to be used carefully, as they can also be intense and overwhelming. I selected yarns that produce toasty snuggly fabrics or are smooth and suitable for summer wear. Similarly, the projects are either winter warmers—some with hoods to add extra warmth—or a sun-top with cutaway shoulders to alleviate the unwelcome heat of summer. The Fair Isle technique doubles up the yarn used in each row, making the fabric extra warm and keeping out breezes. It also produces a very stable fabric suitable for garments when very little else is being worn. Throughout the patterning in these projects there is a gradation in color, an idea drawn from looking at a roaring fire, where the base is darker, moving through each shade to the brighter tip of the licking flames.

# sunkissed

## HALTER TOP

The warmth of the sun on our bodies is one of life's simple pleasures. The first sunny day of the summer lifts our mood and entices us outdoors. The desire to soak up these rays makes people act like flowers, turning to face the sun.

You'll be all set to bare a shoulder on that sunny day or on a sultry summer evening in this halter top. Its colors, drawn from the fire of the sun, are placed in gradually changing hues to mirror the beauty and glow of the setting sun.

### Sizes/Finished Chest Measurements

XS 32½" [82.5cm]

S 34½" [87.5cm]

M 36½" [93cm]

L 40½" [103cm]

XL 42" [106.5cm]

2X 46" [117cm]

Instructions are given for the smallest size. If changes are necessary for larger sizes, the instructions are given in ( ). Where there is only one set of figures, this applies to all sizes.

### Materials

Young Touch Cotton DK by Estelle Designs (100% mercerized cotton; 114yds [105m]/50g ball)

Color A, shade 0116: 2 (2-3-3-3-4) balls

Color B, shade 0059: 2 (2-3-3-3-4) balls

Color C, shade 7565: 1 (1-2-2-2-3) ball

Color D, shade 0111: 2 (2-3-3-3-4) balls

Color E, shade 0019: 1 ball

Color F, shade 0039: 1 ball

Pair each of size 7 [4.5mm] and size 5 [3.75mm] needles, 2 stitch holders

Yarn amounts are based on average requirements and are approximate.

### Gauge

25 sts and 26 rows = 4" [10cm] over Fair Isle patt size 7 [4.5mm] needles

Take time to check your gauge; change the needle sizes if necessary to obtain the correct gauge and garment size.

### Special Instructions

When shaping top, work decs 1 stitch in from edge as follows:

**RS rows:** Work dec at beg of row as ssk, work dec at end of row as k2tog.

**WS rows:** Work dec at beg of row as p2tog, work dec at end of row as p2togb.

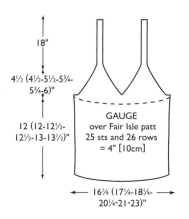

18"

4½ (4½-5½-5¾-5¾-6)"

12 (12-12½-12½-13-13½)"

GAUGE over Fair Isle patt 25 sts and 26 rows = 4" [10cm]

16¼ (17¼-18¼-20¼-21-23)"

## Chart A

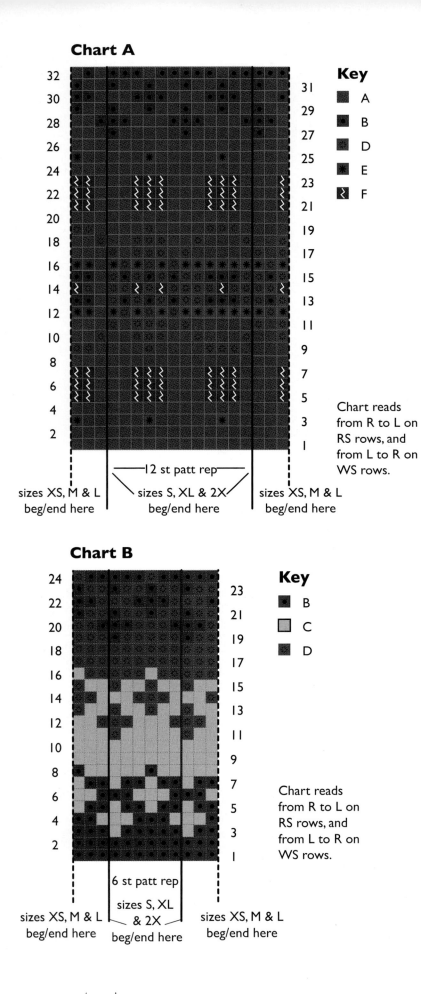

**Key**
- ■ A
- ■ B
- ■ D
- ✳ E
- ⟨ F

12 st patt rep

sizes XS, M & L beg/end here | sizes S, XL & 2X beg/end here | sizes XS, M & L beg/end here

Chart reads from R to L on RS rows, and from L to R on WS rows.

## Chart B

**Key**
- ■ B
- □ C
- ■ D

6 st patt rep
sizes S, XL & 2X beg/end here

sizes XS, M & L beg/end here | | sizes XS, M & L beg/end here

Chart reads from R to L on RS rows, and from L to R on WS rows.

## Front

Using size 7 [4.5mm] needles and Color A, cast on 102 (108-114-126-132-144) sts.

Work in 1 x 1 rib as follows:

**RS row:** (K1, p1) to end.

**WS row:** Rep RS row.

Rep last 2 rows once more.

PLACE FAIR ISLE CHART A AS FOLLOWS:

**RS row:** Following Row 1 Chart A, beg at RHS of chart, work first 3 (0-3-3-0-0) sts as shown, then work 12 st patt rep 8 (9-9-10-11-12) times, 3 (0-3-3-0-0) sts rem, work as shown at LHS of chart.

**WS row:** Following Row 2 Chart A, beg at LHS of chart, work first 3 (0-3-3-0-0) sts as shown, then work 12 st patt rep 8 (9-9-10-11-12) times, 3 (0-3-3-0-0) sts rem, work as shown at RHS of chart.

Fair Isle patt is now set. Work Rows 3–32 Chart A in sequence, changing colors as indicated.

PLACE FAIR ISLE CHART B AS FOLLOWS:

**RS row:** Following Row 1 Chart B, beg at RHS of chart, work first 3 (0-3-3-0-0) sts as shown, then work 6 st patt rep 16 (18-18-20-22-24) times, 3 (0-3-3-0-0) sts rem, work as shown at LHS of chart.

**WS row:** Following Row 2 Chart B, beg at LHS of chart, work first 3 (0-3-3-0-0) sts as shown, then work 6 st patt rep 16 (18-18-20-22-24) times, 3 (0-3-3-0-0) sts rem, work as shown at RHS of chart.

Chart B patt is now set, cont following Chart B only, working rows in sequence, changing colors as indicated, until Front measures 12 (12-12½-12½-13-13½)" [30.5 (30.5-32-32-33-34.5)cm] from beg, end with RS row facing for next row.

SHAPE ARMHOLE AS FOLLOWS:

BO 4 sts at beg of next 2 rows and 0 (3-2-2-3-5) sts at beg of following 2 rows, 94 (94-102-114-118-126) sts rem.

**SHAPE LHS TOP AS FOLLOWS:**
Keeping continuity of patt correct, k1, ssk, work another 42 (42-46-52-54-58) sts, k2tog, turn. Leave rem 47 (47-51-57-59-63) sts on a spare needle for RHS.

Working on sts for LHS only, dec 1 st at each end of following 9 (9-7-11-13-15) rows, 27 (27-35-33-31-31) sts rem (see note on decs). Then dec 1 st at each end of every following RS row 10 (10-14-13-12-12) times, 7 sts rem. Leave these sts on a st holder for strap.

**SHAPE RHS TOP AS FOLLOWS:**
Return to sts on spare needle. Rejoin yarn, ssk, work in patt to last 3 sts, k2tog, k1.

Dec 1 st at each end of following 9 (9-7-11-13-15) rows, 27 (27-35-33-31-31) sts rem. Then dec 1 st at each end of every following RS row 10 (10-14-13-12-12) times, 7 sts rem. Leave these sts on a st holder for strap.

## Back

Work as given for Front until beg of armhole shaping.

Using Color D, work 2 rows in 1 x 1 rib as given for lower edge of Front. BO all sts in rib using size 5 [3.75mm] needle.

## Finishing and Straps

Using size 5 [3.75mm] needles and Color D, with RS facing pick up and knit 40 (42-46-48-50-54) sts along armhole edge of LHS front top shaping. BO all sts.

Rep for RHS armhole.

Using size 5 [3.75mm] needles and Color B, with RS facing pick up and knit 60 (62-70-74-74-78) sts along V-neck. BO all sts.

Using size 5 [3.75mm] needles and Color B, return to 7 sts for strap, work these in 1 x 1 rib until strap measures 18" [46cm]. BO all sts. Rep for second strap.

Sew in all ends. Block pieces to given measurements.

Join side seams.

Press lightly, following the instructions on the yarn label.

## beltane

Beltane was a symbolic Gaelic festival celebrating the ease of summer over the struggle of winter. The use of fire in this festival speaks of both practicality and of superstitions indicating a belief that the heat of the summer months kept evil spirits at bay. To pay tribute to the fire god and to bring good fortune, cattle were driven between pairs of bonfires so that the purifying heat would remove winter diseases and keep the milk from being stolen by evil spirits. Six months later, at summer's end when the heat subsides, the spirits rose once again at Halloween.

# hearth

## MEN'S YOKE-PATTERNED SWEATER

The energy associated with fire can be thought of as both localized and spreading or dissipating. Heat and light from fire radiates away from its source so that it feels hotter and more brilliant the closer you are to it. When we are cold, the instinct to huddle close to a fire or heater is great. As we soak up the heat and comfort spreads through our limbs, this desire wanes.

A simplified depiction of the shape of a flame becomes the zigzag pattern used in the Fair Isle at the yoke in this sweater. The changing colors are placed in a slowly ascending order from coolest to warmest, also darkest to lightest, chosen to illustrate that the tip of a flame is brighter than its base.

### Sizes/Finished Chest Measurements

XS 43" [109cm]

S 46" [117cm]

M 49" [124.5cm]

L 52" [132cm]

XL 55" [140cm]

Instructions are given for the smallest size. If changes are necessary for larger sizes, the instructions are given in ( ). Where there is only one set of figures, this applies to all sizes.

### Materials

Cascade 220 by Cascade Yarns (100% wool; 220yds [201 m]/100g skein)

M/C, shade 2403: 6 (6-7-8-8) skeins

Color A, shade 8021: 1 (1-2-2) skein

Color B, shade 2401: 1 (1-2-2) skein

Color C, shade 2415: 1 (1-2-2) skein

Pair each of size 5 [3.75mm] needles, size 6 [4mm] needles and size 7 [4.5mm] needles; size 5 [3.75mm] circular needle for neckband, 3 stitch holders

Yarn amounts given are based on average requirements and are approximate.

### Gauge

21 sts and 22 rows = 4" [10cm] over Fair Isle patt size 7 [4.5mm] needles

21 sts and 26 rows = 4" [10cm] over St st on size 6 [4mm] needles

Take the time to check your gauge; change the needle size if necessary to obtain the correct gauge and garment size.

REFER TO GLOSSARY ON PAGE 23 FOR: **Seed Stitch**

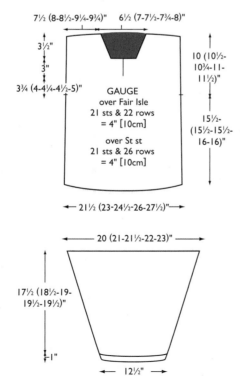

7½ (8-8½-9¼-9¾)"     6½ (7-7½-7¾-8)"

3½"

3"

3¾ (4-4¼-4½-5)"

GAUGE
over Fair Isle
21 sts & 22 rows
= 4" [10cm]

over St st
21 sts & 26 rows
= 4" [10cm]

10 (10½-10¾-11-11½)"

15½-(15½-15½-16-16)"

21½ (23-24½-26-27½)"

20 (21-21½-22-23)"

17½ (18½-19-19½-19½)"

12½"

1"

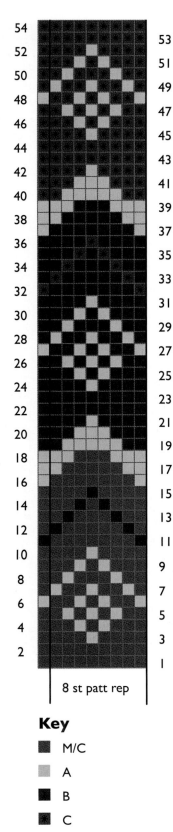

Left side row numbers (top to bottom): 54, 52, 50, 48, 46, 44, 42, 40, 38, 36, 34, 32, 30, 28, 26, 24, 22, 20, 18, 16, 14, 12, 10, 8, 6, 4, 2

Right side row numbers (top to bottom): 53, 51, 49, 47, 45, 43, 41, 39, 37, 35, 33, 31, 29, 27, 25, 23, 21, 19, 17, 15, 13, 11, 9, 7, 5, 3, 1

8 st patt rep

## Key

■ M/C
■ A
■ B
■ C

Chart reads from R to L on RS rows, and from L to R on WS rows.

## Back

Using size 5 [3.75mm] needles and M/C, cast on 113 (121-129-137-145) sts. Work 6 rows in seed st.

Change to size 6 [4mm] needles, beg with a knit row, work in St st until Back measures 15½ (15½-15½-16-16)" [39 (39-39-40.5-40.5)cm], end with RS row facing for next row.

Change to size 7 [4.5mm] needles.

### PLACE FAIR ISLE PATTERN AS FOLLOWS:
RS row: Following Row 1 and beg at RHS of chart, work 8 st patt 14 (15-16-17-18) times, 1 st rem, work as shown at LHS of chart.

WS row: Following Row 2 and beg at LHS of chart, work first st as shown, then work 8 st patt rep 14 (15-16-17-18) times.

Fair Isle patt is now set. Cont working chart Rows 3–54 in sequence, changing colors as indicated.

Change back to size 6 [4mm] needles and beg with a knit row work in St st using Color C until Back measures 25½ (26-26¼-27-27½)" [65 (66-66.5-67-70)cm] from cast-on edge, end with RS row facing for next row.

### SHAPE SHOULDER AS FOLLOWS:
Cont in St st, BO 13 (14-15-16-17) sts at beg of next 6 rows. Leave rem 35 (37-39-41-43) sts on a st holder for back neck.

## Front

Work as given for Back until Fair Isle chart has been placed. Work following chart until row 20 (22-24-26-28) of chart has been completed, work will measure approx 19 (19½-19¾-20¾-21)" [48.5 (49.5-50-52.5-53.5)cm].

### DIVIDE FOR CF OPENING AS FOLLOWS:
Cont in Fair Isle patt as set, work 56 (60-64-68-72) sts, place next st on a st holder, join second ball(s) of yarn to rem 56 (60-64-68-72) sts, and work in patt to end. Cont in patt, working both sides of front separately until CF opening measures 3" [7.5cm] from beg of divide, end with RS row facing

for next row.

### SHAPE LH FRONT NECK AS FOLLOWS:
During front neck shaping, cont working from chart until row 54 is complete, then change to size 6 [4mm] needles and beg with a knit row, work in St st using Color C throughout.

RS row: Work across 49 (52-57-60-63) sts, turn, leave next 7 (8-7-8-9) sts on a stitch holder for front neck. Leave rem 56 (60-64-68-72) sts on a spare needle for RHS.

Working on the LHS sts only, keeping continuity of patt correct, dec 1 st at neck edge on the next 10 (10-12-12-12) rows, 39 (42-45-48-51) sts rem. Work even until Front measures the same as Back before shoulder shaping, end with RS row facing for next row.

### SHAPE LH SHOULDER AS FOLLOWS:
BO 13 (14-15-16-17) sts at beg of row, work in patt to end. Work WS row even.

Rep last 2 rows once more. BO rem 13 (14-15-16-17) sts.

### SHAPE RH FRONT NECK AS FOLLOWS:
Return to sts on spare needle for RHS, slip first 7 (8-7-8-9) sts onto a stitch holder, rejoin yarn, work in patt to end.

Keeping continuity of patt correct, dec 1 st at neck edge on the next 10 (10-12-12-12) rows, 39 (42-45-48-51) sts rem. Work even until Front measures the same as Back before shoulder shaping, end with WS row facing for next row.

### SHAPE RH SHOULDER AS FOLLOWS:
BO 13 (14-15-16-17) sts at beg of row, work in patt to end. Work RS row even.

Rep last 2 rows once more. BO rem 13 (14-15-16-17) sts.

## Sleeve (Make 2)

Using size 5 [3.75mm] needles and M/C, cast on 66 sts, work 6 rows in seed st.

Change to size 6 [4mm] needles and beg with a knit row, work in St st throughout, *at the same time* inc 1 st at each end of row 5 and every following 6th row 13 (12-12-9-5) times, 94 (92-92-86-78) sts. Then inc 1 st at each end of every 4th row 6 (9-10-15-21) times, 106 (110-112-116-120) sts.

Work even until Sleeve measures 18½ (19½-20-20½-20½)" [47 (49.5-51-52-52)cm] from cast-on edge. BO all sts loosely.

## Finishing and Neckband

Sew in all ends. Block pieces to given dimensions.

Join both shoulder seams.

Using size 5 [3.75mm] needles and Color B, with RS facing pick up and knit 15 sts down left of CF opening, knit st from CF stitch holder, then pick up and knit 15 sts up right of CF opening, 31 sts. BO all sts loosely.

Using circular size 5 [3.75mm] needle and Color C, with RS facing beg at CF knit across 7 (8-7-8-9) sts from right front neck stitch holder, then pick up and knit 27 sts up right front neck, knit across 35 (37-39-41-43) sts from back neck stitch holder, then pick up and knit 27 sts down left front neck, knit across 7 (8-7-8-9) sts from left front neck stitch holder, 103

(107-107-111-115) sts. Working back and forth work 4 rows in seed st. BO all sts loosely in patt.

Place markers on all side seams 10 (10½-10¾-11-11½)" [25.5 (26.5-27-28-29)cm] down from each shoulder seam to indicate placement for setting in Sleeves. Sew in Sleeves between markers.

Sew side and Sleeve seams.

Press lightly, following instructions on the yarn label.

## aztec creation story

According to Aztec belief, there were five cycles, or ages, of creation, each accompanied by a different sun. The Aztecs believed they were living in the fifth age at the time of their empire's demise.

In this final age, the sun was created by fire. An earthbound spirit was tricked into sacrificing himself to produce the new sun. After he entered the flames, the other spirits waited to see where the sun would rise in the sky. He appeared, and was so brilliant that nobody could look at him. He remained high in the sky and didn't move, scorching everything on Earth. The spirits sent up a falcon to find out why he didn't move. He answered that he would not move until the other spirits also sacrificed themselves. The spirits asked the morning star to shoot the sun with his arrows, but the sun dodged them and shot back flame-colored darts that wounded the morning star. Finally, the spirits realized that the sun's power couldn't be resisted, so they sacrificed themselves. Satisfied, the sun finally continued his journey across the sky.

# glowing

## WOMEN'S RAGLAN SWEATER

We often think of fire as being overpowering and destructive, but it can also be very reassuring and comforting. Hours can be whiled away watching flames flicker and dance, and many good stories have been told (and marshmallows roasted) while gazing into the soft glow of a hearth or campfire. Even dying flames contain some of that initial intensity and also the potential to reignite and burn ferociously.

 This hooded sweater draws its graphic patterning from simplified and stylized flames, its colors from the glow of embers. Worked in the round, the easy-to-follow patterning will radiate contentment while you're knitting and its easy shaping will make it comforting to wear.

### Sizes/Finished Chest Measurements

S 35" [89cm]

M 38" [96.5cm]

L 41" [104cm]

XL 44" [112cm]

2X 46½" [118cm]

3X 49½" [126cm]

Instructions are given for the smallest size. If changes are necessary for larger sizes, the instructions are given in ( ). Where there is only one set of figures, this applies to all sizes.

### Materials

1824 Wool by Mission Falls (100% wool; 85 yds [78m]/50 g ball)

M/C, shade Raspberry 029: 11 (12-13-15-16-17) balls

Color A, shade Rhubarb 0534: 2 (2-2-3-3-3) balls

Color B, shade Damson 024: 4 (4-4-5-5-5) balls

Color C, shade Squash 0533: 1 (1-1-2-2-2) balls

Color D, shade Teal 030: 1 (1-2-2-2-3) balls

Color E, shade Pistachio 028: 1 (1-1-1-2-2) balls

Size 8 [5mm] circular needle, (24" [61cm] long), circular size 7 [4.5mm] needles (one 24" [61cm] long and one 20" [51cm] long), sets of size 7 [4.5mm] and size 8 [5mm] dpns, 4 stitch holders

Yarn amounts given are based on average requirements and are approximate.

### Gauge

17 sts and 20 rnds = 4" [10cm] over Fair Isle patt on circular size 8 [5mm] needle

Take the time to check your gauge; change the needle size if necessary to obtain the correct gauge and garment size.

REFER TO THINGS YOU NEED TO KNOW ON PAGE 14 FOR: **Working In the Round**

REFER TO TECHNIQUES ON PAGE 18 FOR: **3-Needle Bind Off**

REFER TO GLOSSARY ON PAGE 23 FOR: **Seed Stitch**

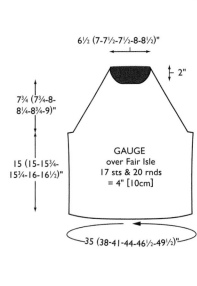

6½ (7-7½-7½-8-8½)"

‡ 2"

7¾ (7¾-8-8¼-8¾-9)"

GAUGE
over Fair Isle
17 sts & 20 rnds
= 4" [10cm]

15 (15-15¾-15¾-16-16½)"

35 (38-41-44-46½-49½)"

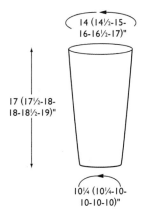

14 (14½-15-16-16½-17)"

17 (17½-18-18-18½-19)"

10¼ (10¼-10-10-10-10)"

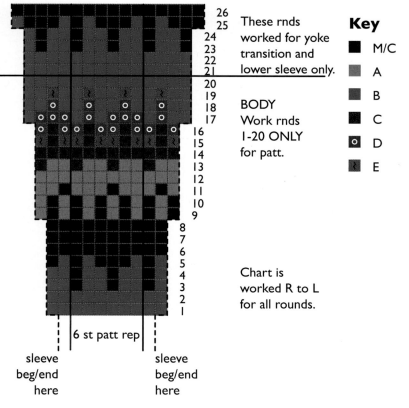

26
25
24
23
22
21
20
19
18
17
16
15
14
13
12
11
10
9
8
7
6
5
4
3
2
1

These rnds worked for yoke transition and lower sleeve only.

BODY
Work rnds 1-20 ONLY for patt.

**Key**

- ■ M/C
- ▪ A
- ▪ B
- ■ C
- ▣ D
- ▨ E

Chart is worked R to L for all rounds.

6 st patt rep

sleeve beg/end here

sleeve beg/end here

## Body

Using longer size 7 [4.5mm] circular needle and Color B, cast on 138 (150-162-172-184-194) sts. Place marker to indicate beg of rnd and join, being careful not to twist. Work 2 rnds in seed st. Cont in St st, work 6 (6-10-10-12-14) rnds in Color B, inc 12 (12-12-14-14-16) sts evenly on last rnd, 150 (162-174-186-198-210) sts.

Change to circular size 8 [5mm] needle and beg with Rnd 1 of chart, work 6 st patt rep 25 (27-29-31-33-35) times across rnd. Cont working chart rnds in sequence, changing colors as indicated, work Rnds 1–20 three times plus Rnds 21–26, Body will now measure approx 15 (15-15¾-15¾-16-16½)" [38 (38-40-40-40.5-42)cm] from beg.

Change to longer size 7 [4.5mm] needle and, using M/C, knit 1 rnd until 5 sts before marker. BO next 10 sts, k65 (71-77-83-89-95), BO next 10 sts, knit to end.

Place each set of 65 (71-77-83-89-95) sts on separate stitch holders for front and back.

## Sleeve (Make 2)

Using size 7 [4.5mm] dpns and Color B, cast on 36 (36-34-34-34-34) sts. Place marker to indicate beg of rnd and join, being careful not to twist.

Work 2 rnds in seed st, inc 8 sts evenly on last rnd, 44 (44-42-42-42-42) sts.

Working in the rnd and in St st, work 6 (6-4-4-6-2) rnds in Color B.

SIZES L, XL, 2X AND 3X ONLY:
**Next rnd:** K1, m1, knit to last st before marker, m1, k1, 44 sts. Work another 5 (5-5-7) rnds using Color B.

ALL SIZES:
Change to size 8 [5mm] dpns and beg with Rnd 1 of chart where indicated for Sleeve, work 1 st, m1, work 6 st patt rep 7 times, m1, work last st.

Work following chart rnds in sequence, changing colors as indicated, *at the same time* inc 1 st each side of marker, as before, on Rnds 9, 17, and 25 of chart as shown, 52 sts. Work Rnd 26 of chart.

Change to size 7 [4.5mm] dpns, and using M/C, work in St st throughout. Inc 1 st each side of marker as

before every 12 (10-8-6-6-6)th rnd 4 (5-2-8-6-7) times, 60 (62-56-68-64-66) sts. Then inc 1 st each side of marker every 0 (0-6-0-4-4)th rnd 0 (0-5-0-3-3) times, 60 (62-66-68-70-72) sts. Work all inc sts in St st.

Work even until Sleeve measures 17 (17½-18-18-18½-19)" [43 (44.5-45.5-45.5-47-48.5)cm] from cast-on edge, ending last rnd 5 sts before marker.

**Next rnd:** BO 10 sts, knit to end.

Leave rem 50 (52-56-58-60-62) sts on a stitch holder.

## Yoke

JOIN BODY AND SLEEVES AS FOLLOWS:
Using shorter size 7 [4.5mm] needle, and M/C, beg with sts for left sleeve, place marker, k1, place marker, knit rem 49 (51-55-57-59-61) sts from sleeve stitch holder, place marker, k1 from sts held for front, place marker, knit rem 64 (70-76-82-88-94) sts from front stitch holder, place marker, k1 from sts held for right sleeve, place marker, knit rem 49 (51-55-57-59-61) sts from sleeve stitch holder, place marker, k1 from sts held for back, place marker, knit rem 64 (70-76-82-88-94) sts from back stitch holder, 230 (246-266-282-298-314) sts total.

Work 1 rnd even.

**Dec rnd:** Slip first marker, *k1, slip marker, ssk, work to 2 sts before next marker, k2tog, slip marker; rep from * 3 times, 8 sts have been dec, 222 (238-258-274-290-306) sts rem.

Work 1 rnd even.

Rep last 2 rnds 14 (14-15-15-16-16) more times, 110 (126-138-154-162-178) sts rem.

SHAPE FRONT NECK AS FOLLOWS:
**Next rnd:** *K1, slip marker, ssk, work to 2 sts before next marker, k2tog, slip marker,* k1, slip marker, ssk, k9 (10-11-15-15-19) sts, break off yarn, slip next 12 (16-18-16-20-18) sts onto a stitch holder for front neck, rejoin yarn, k9 (10-11-15-15-19), k2tog, slip marker, rep from * to * twice, 90 (102-112-130-134-152) sts rem.

**Next rnd:** Work even to front neck, turn work.

**SMALL AND MEDIUM SIZES ONLY:**
Working back and forth in rows, work decs as established on either side of markers on next RS row, then work decs (as established) on every following 4th row twice, *at the same time* dec 1 at each side of front neck every row 3 (7) times, 60 (64) sts rem.

**LARGE, XL, 2X AND 3X SIZES ONLY:**
Working back and forth in rows, work decs as established on either side of markers on next 4 (3-4-4) RS rows, then work dec (as established) on following 0 (3-2-4) rows *at the same time* dec 1 at each side of front neck every row 7 (9-9-11) times, leave rem 66 (64-68-66) sts on a spare needle.

## Hood

Beg at top of left front neck shaping with RS facing using shorter size 7 [4.5mm] needle and M/C, pick up and knit 8 (8-8-10-10-12) sts down left front neck, then knit across first 6 (8-9-8-10-9) sts from front neck st holder, leave these 14 (16-17-18-20-21) sts on a spare needle. Leave rem 6 (8-9-8-10-9) sts on front neck st holder.

Beg at CF, using shorter size 7 [4.5mm] needle and M/C, knit across rem 6 (8-9-8-10-9) sts from front neck stitch holder, then pick up and knit 8 (8-8-10-10-12) sts up right front neck. Cont working across 60 (64-66-64-68-66) sts on spare needle from yoke. Work across 14 (16-17-18-20-21) sts on spare needle from left front neck, 88 (96-100-100-108-108) sts total.

**WORK BACK AND FORTH IN ROWS AS FOLLOWS:**
**RS rows:** Knit.

**WS rows:** K4, purl to last 4 sts, k4.

Rep last 2 rows until Hood measures 11" [28cm] from pick-up row, end with RS row facing for next row.

**SHAPE TOP OF HOOD AS FOLLOWS:**
**RS row:** K23 (27-29-29-33-33), k2tog, place marker, k1, ssk, k13, k2tog, place marker, (ssk) twice, k13, k2tog, place marker, k1, ssk, knit to end, 81 (89-93-93-101-101) sts rem.

**WS row:** K4, purl to last 4 sts, k4.

**Next RS row:** *Knit to 2 sts before marker, k2tog, slip marker, k1, ssk; rep from * twice more, knit to end.

Rep last 2 rows 4 more times, 51 (59-63-63-71-71) sts rem.

Divide rem sts evenly onto 2 needles (1 needle will have an extra st), with RS tog BO all sts using the 3-needle bind-off method (work last 2 sts tog on needle with extra st).

## Finishing

Sew in all ends. Block garment to given dimensions. Join armholes below Yoke.

Press lightly, following the instructions given on the yarn label.

# glassmaking

All four of the elements have the ability to perform spectacular acts of transformation, but they never seem to work independently; one is generally the dominant force. Lightning striking sand can form glass without any human intervention. When humans harness fire, breath, and the basic raw materials necessary to create glass, they elevate its creation to an art form.

Glassmaking was once surrounded in mystery and was sometimes considered alchemy. When we see an artist take silica, alkali, and lime, add the all-important heat from a furnace, then add his breath, the transformation that takes place is indeed magical. An object of beauty is created that, because of its delicacy and transparency, appears to hardly exist. I must admit that this use of fire appears even more magical to me than turning raw yarn into a knitted piece.

# kindle

## MUFFLER

Sometimes the elements work in tandem to provide life's basic essentials. The warmth provided by fire can be necessary to protect us against harsh winter chills. But it's not practical to have a fire wherever we go, so we have devised ways to trap this warmth into our clothing through pockets of air. The fluffier a yarn, the more air is trapped between its fibers, and its ability to keep us warm is thus increased. Using two strands of yarn produces a double layer of fabric, creating lots of pockets of air for insulation.

This Fair Isle pattern is knitted horizontally, its spiky motifs, reminiscent of fireworks, set on a diagonal to give the impression of a spiral; the apparent upward movement reminding us of the fact that heat rises.

### Finished Measurements

Muffler measures 18" [45.5cm] around and 54" [137cm] long.

### Materials

Sport Weight Alpaca by Blue Sky Alpacas (100% alpaca; 110yds [100m]/50g skein)

M/C, shade 511: 5 skeins

Color A, shade 504: 4 skeins

Color B, shade 521: 1 skein

Size 7 [4.5mm] circular needle 16" [40.5cm] long, pair of size 7 [4.5mm] dpns

### Gauge

27 sts and 26 rnds = 4" [10cm] over Fair Isle pattern on size 7 [4.5mm] circular needle

Take the time to check your gauge; change the needle size if necessary to obtain the correct gauge and garment size.

REFER TO THINGS YOU NEED TO KNOW ON PAGE 14 FOR: **Working in the Round**

REFER TO TECHNIQUES ON PAGE 18 FOR: **I-Cord**

REFER TO GLOSSARY ON PAGE 23 FOR: **Garter Ridge**

Using size 7 [4.5mm] circular needle and M/C, cast on 99 sts. Place marker to indicate beg of rnd. Take care not to twist, join in the rnd and knit 1 rnd, purl 1 rnd (produces garter ridge).

**Eyelet rnd (RS):** *K1, yfon, k2tog, rep from * to end.

Knit 2 rnds, inc 21 sts evenly on last rnd, 120 sts.

### PLACE FAIR ISLE PATT A AS FOLLOWS:
Following Rnd 1, Chart A, beg at RHS
of chart, work 24 st patt rep 5 times across rnd.

Work Rnds 2–24 Chart A in sequence changing colors as indicated.

Change to Color B, knit 1 rnd, purl 1 rnd (garter ridge).

### PLACE FAIR ISLE PATT B AS FOLLOWS:
Following Rnd 1, Chart B, beg at
RHS of chart, work 24 st patt rep 5 times across rnd.

Work Rnds 2–12 Chart B in sequence.

Using Color B, knit 1 rnd, purl 1 rnd (garter ridge).

### PLACE FAIR ISLE PATT C AS FOLLOWS:
Following Rnd 1 Chart C, beg at RHS of chart, work 24 st patt rep 5 times across rnd.

Work Rnds 2–24 Chart C in sequence followed by Rnds 1–24 10 more times.

Using Color B knit 1 rnd, purl 1 rnd (garter ridge).

### PLACE FAIR ISLE PATT D AS FOLLOWS:
Following Rnd 1 Chart D, beg at RHS of Chart, work 24 st patt rep 5 times across rnd.

Work Rnds 2–12 Chart D in sequence.

Using Color B knit 1 rnd, purl 1 rnd, (garter ridge).

### PLACE FAIR ISLE PATT E AS FOLLOWS:
Following Rnd 1 Chart E, beg at RHS of chart, work 24 st patt rep 5 times across rnd.

Work Rnds 2–24 Chart E in sequence.

Change to M/C, knit 2 rnds, dec 21 sts evenly across 2nd rnd, 99 sts.

Work Eyelet rnd as given above.

Knit 1 rnd, purl 1 rnd, (garter ridge). BO all sts purlwise.

### MAKE I-CORDS AS FOLLOWS:
Using size 7 [4.5mm] dpns and Color B, make two 4 st I-cords 70" [178cm] long.

Working through both layers of muffler together, thread I-cords through eyelet holes at each end of the scarf, making fringe, and secure by sewing in place.

Press lightly, following the instructions on the yarn label.

## Chart A

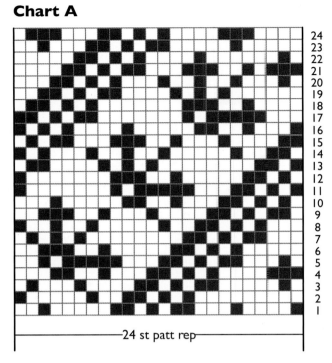

24
23
22
21
20
19
18
17
16
15
14
13
12
11
10
9
8
7
6
5
4
3
2
1

—24 st patt rep—

**Key**

■ M/C

□ A

Chart reads from R to L
for all rounds.

## Chart B

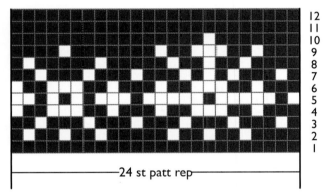

12
11
10
9
8
7
6
5
4
3
2
1

—24 st patt rep—

**Key**

□ A

■ B

Chart reads from R to L
for all rounds.

## Chart C

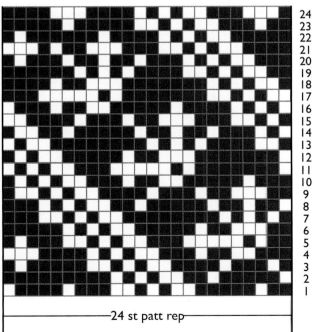

24
23
22
21
20
19
18
17
16
15
14
13
12
11
10
9
8
7
6
5
4
3
2
1

—24 st patt rep—

**Key**

■ M/C

□ A

Chart reads from R to L
for all rounds.

**Chart D**

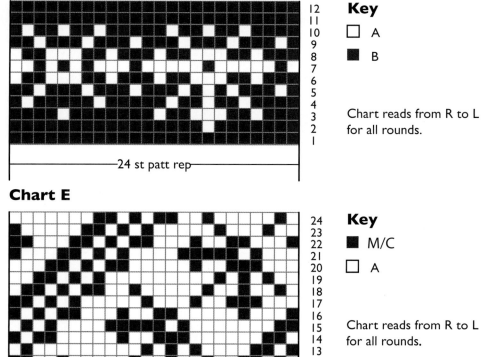

12
11
10
9
8
7
6
5
4
3
2
1

—24 st patt rep—

**Key**

☐ A

■ B

Chart reads from R to L
for all rounds.

**Chart E**

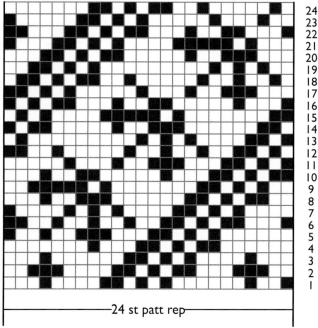

24
23
22
21
20
19
18
17
16
15
14
13
12
11
10
9
8
7
6
5
4
3
2
1

—24 st patt rep—

**Key**

■ M/C

☐ A

Chart reads from R to L
for all rounds.

# fire in festivals

Throughout time, the elements have been incorporated into many festive situations where they often play a leading role. Glancing through the indices of books about festivals, holidays, and folklore reveals fire to be the most widely used element.

In Britain, the discovery of a plot to blow up the Parliament in 1605 is still celebrated every November 5 by burning an effigy on a bonfire. There are also many festivals of light where lanterns were originally lit to honor gods, ward off evil spirits, or light the way for souls returning from or on the journey toward the underworld. Sometimes the original meanings have been lost, but the rituals are still performed. Candles abound in religious ceremonies, and fire is often used symbolically, as an eternal flame burning at a monument, or as a torch linking modernity to antiquity at the Olympic games.

# toasty

## KIDS' ZIPPERED CARDIGAN

The elements all have color associations and, of course, fire is an easy one to define. Colors are often described in terms of their color temperature—being either warm or cool. But how warm or cool a color appears is dependent on the colors around it—a subjective assessment. Orange, a true fire color, should be used sparingly, as it is made up of two already warm colors, yellow and red, and can be a little too hot to handle in large areas.

Inspired by playful dancing flames, this zippered hoodie's Fair Isle patterns and stripes place cool hues next to warmer ones to heat them up. Plenty of orange is included so kids will look as toasty in this garment as they feel.

## Sizes/Finished Chest Measurements

XS 28" [71cm]

S 30" [76cm]

M 32" [81cm]

L 34" [86cm]

XL 38" [96.5cm]

Instructions are given for the smallest size. If changes are necessary for larger sizes, the instructions are given in ( ). Where there is only one set of figures, this applies to all sizes.

## Materials

Falk by Dale of Norway (100% wool, 116yds [106m]/50g ball)

M/C, shade 3418: 3 (3-3-4-4) balls

Color A, shade 2427: 2 (2-3-3-3) balls

Color B, shade 9155: 1 (1-1-2-2) balls

Color C, shade 3727: 2 (2-2-2-3) balls

Color D, shade 5224: 1 (1-2-2-2) balls

Color E, shade 5036: 2 (2-3-3-3) balls

Color F, shade 4018: 1 (1-2-2-3) balls

Color G, shade 9834: 1 (1-1-1-2) balls

Pair each of size 6 [4mm] and size 7 [4.5mm] needles, 3 stitch holders, one 12 (14-14-14-16)" [30.5 (35.5-35.5-35.5-40.5)cm] long zipper.

Yarn amounts given are based on average requirements and are approximate.

## Gauge

24 sts and 26 rows = 4" [10cm] over Fair Isle patt on size 7 [4.5mm] needles

22 sts and 30 rows = 4" [10cm] over St st on size 6 [4mm] needles

Take the time to check your gauge; change the needle size if necessary to obtain the correct gauge and garment size.

REFER TO TECHNIQUES ON PAGE 18 FOR: **Setting In a Zipper**

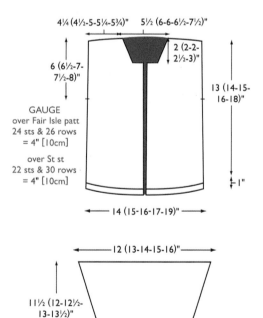

4¼ (4½-5-5¼-5¾)"     5½ (6-6-6½-7½)"

2 (2-2-2½-3)"

6 (6½-7-7½-8)"

13 (14-15-16-18)"

GAUGE
over Fair Isle patt
24 sts & 26 rows
= 4" [10cm]

over St st
22 sts & 30 rows
= 4" [10cm]

1"

14 (15-16-17-19)"

12 (13-14-15-16)"

11½ (12-12½-13-13½)"

1"

7½ (8¾-8¾-9¾-9¾)"

## Chart A

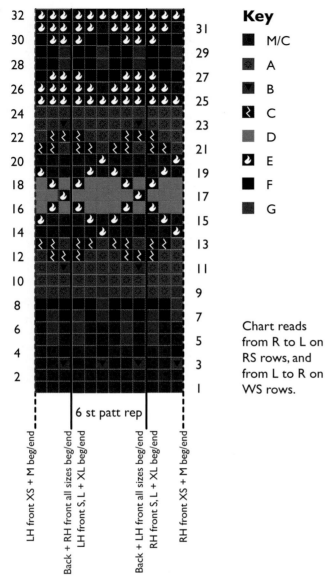

Row numbers on left: 32, 30, 28, 26, 24, 22, 20, 18, 16, 14, 12, 10, 8, 6, 4, 2

Row numbers on right: 31, 29, 27, 25, 23, 21, 19, 17, 15, 13, 11, 9, 7, 5, 3, 1

**Key**

- ■ M/C
- ▩ A
- ▼ B
- ⟩ C
- ▦ D
- ⟩ E
- ■ F
- ▦ G

Chart reads from R to L on RS rows, and from L to R on WS rows.

6 st patt rep

LH front XS + M beg/end
Back + RH front all sizes beg/end
LH front S, L + XL beg/end
Back + LH front all sizes beg/end
RH front S, L + XL beg/end
RH front XS + M beg/end

## Chart B

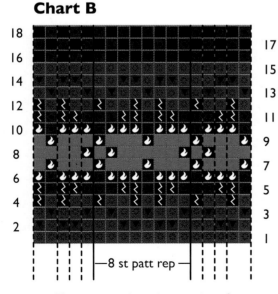

Row numbers on left: 18, 16, 14, 12, 10, 8, 6, 4, 2

Row numbers on right: 17, 15, 13, 11, 9, 7, 5, 3, 1

**Key**

- ■ M/C
- ▩ A
- ▼ B
- ⟩ C
- ▦ D
- ⟩ E
- ■ F

8 st patt rep

Please see written instructions for beg/end for sizes.

Chart reads from R to L on RS rows, and from L to R on WS rows.

## Stripe Sequence

3 rows Color A

1 row Color B

2 rows Color C

1 row M/C

1 row Color E

1 row Color D

2 rows Color E

1 row Color F

2 rows M/C

## Back

Using size 7 [4.5mm] needles and M/C, cast on 84 (90-96-102-114) sts. Work in rib as follows:

**Row 1 (RS):** (K3, p3) to end.

**Row 2:** Rep Row 1.

Rep these 2 rows twice more (6 rows total).

PLACE FAIR ISLE PATT A AS FOLLOWS:
**\*\*RS row:** Following Row 1 Chart A, beg at RHS of chart, work 6 st patt rep 14 (15-16-17-19) times across row.

**WS row:** Following Row 2 Chart A, beg at LHS of chart, work 6 st patt rep 14 (15-16-17-19) times across row.

Cont working Rows 3–32 Chart A in sequence as set, changing colors as indicated.

PLACE FAIR ISLE PATT B AS FOLLOWS:
**RS row:** Following Row 1 Chart B, beg at RHS of chart, work first 2 (1-0-3-1) sts as shown, then work 8 st patt rep 10 (11-12-12-14) times, 2 (1-0-3-1) sts rem, work as shown at LHS of chart.

**WS row:** Following Row 2 Chart B, beg at LHS of chart, work first 2 (1-0-3-1) sts as shown, then work 8 st patt rep 10 (11-12-12-14) times, 2 (1-0-3-1) sts rem, work as shown at RHS of chart.

Cont working Rows 3–18 Chart B in sequence as set.\*\*

Cont working Chart A followed by Chart B (50 row rep) as given from \*\*

to ** until Back measures 13 (14-15-16-18)" [33 (35.5-38-40.5-45.5)cm] from top of rib, end with RS row facing for next row.

**SHAPE SHOULDERS AS FOLLOWS:**
Cont in patt sequence as set, BO 8 (9-10-10-11) sts at beg of next 4 rows, and 9 (9-10-11-12) sts at beg of following 2 rows. Place rem 34 (36-36-40-46) sts on a stitch holder.

## Right Front

Using size 7 [4.5mm] needles and M/C, cast on 39 (42-45-48-54) sts. Work in rib as follows:

**Row 1 (RS):** (K3, p3) to last 3 (0-3-0-0) sts, k3 (k0-k3-k0-k0).

**Row 2:** P3 (p0-p3-p0-p0), (k3, p3) to end.

Rep these 2 rows twice more (6 rows total).

**PLACE FAIR ISLE PATT A AS FOLLOWS:**
**\*\*RS row:** Following Row 1 Chart A, beg at RHS of chart, work first 3 (0-3-0-0) sts as shown, then work 6 st patt rep 6 (7-7-8-9) times.

**WS row:** Following Row 2 Chart A, beg at LHS of chart, work 6 st patt rep 6 (7-7-8-9) times, 3 (0-3-0-0) sts rem, work as shown at RHS of chart.

Cont working Rows 3–32 Chart A as set.

**PLACE FAIR ISLE PATT B AS FOLLOWS:**
**RS row:** Following Row 1 Chart B, beg at RHS of chart, work first 5 (1-3-3-1) sts as shown, then work 8 st patt rep 4 (5-5-5-6) times, 2 (1-2-5-5) sts rem, work as shown at LHS of chart.

**WS row:** Following Row 2 Chart B, beg at LHS of chart, work first 2 (1-2-5-5) sts as shown, then work 8 st patt rep 4 (5-5-5-6) times, 5 (1-3-3-1) sts rem, work as shown at RHS of chart.

Cont working rows 3–18 Chart B as set.\*\*

Cont working Chart A followed by Chart B (50 row rep) as given from ** to ** until Right Front measures 11 (12-13-13½-15)" [28 (30.5-33-34.5-38)cm] from top of rib, end with WS row facing for next row.

**SHAPE FRONT NECK AS FOLLOWS:**
Work in patt to last 5 sts, turn (this is neck edge). Leave rem 5 sts on a st holder. Cont in patt, dec 1 st at neck edge on next 9 (10-10-12-15) rows, 25 (27-30-31-34) sts rem. Work even in patt until Right Front measures the same as Back before shoulder shaping, end with WS row facing for next row.

**SHAPE SHOULDER AS FOLLOWS:**
Cont in patt, BO 8 (9-10-10-11) sts at beg of next row. Work RS row even.

Rep last 2 rows once more. BO rem 9 (9-10-11-12) sts.

## Left Front

Using size 7 [4.5mm] needles and M/C, cast on 39 (42-45-48-54) sts. Work in rib as given for Right Front.

**PLACE FAIR ISLE PATT A AS FOLLOWS:**
**\*\*RS row:** Following Row 1 Chart A, beg at RHS of chart, work 6 st patt rep 6 (7-7-8-9) times, 3 (0-3-0-0) sts rem, work these as shown at LHS of chart.

**WS row:** Following Row 2 Chart A, beg at LHS of chart, work first 3 (0-3-0-0) sts as shown, then work 6 st patt rep 6 (7-7-8-9) times.

Cont working Rows 3–32 Chart A as set.

**PLACE FAIR ISLE PATT B AS FOLLOWS:**
**RS row:** Following Row 1 Chart B, beg at RHS of chart, work first 2 (1-2-5-5) sts as shown, then work 8 st patt rep 4 (5-5-5-6) times, 5 (1-3-3-1) sts rem, work as shown at LHS of chart.

**WS row:** Following Row 2 Chart B, beg at LHS of chart, work first 5 (1-3-3-1) sts as shown, then work 8 st patt rep 4 (5-5-5-6) times, 2 (1-2-5-5)

98 toasty

sts rem, work as shown at RHS of chart.

Cont working Rows 3–18 Chart B as set.**

Cont working Chart A followed by Chart B (50 row rep) as given from ** to ** until Left Front measures 11 (12-13-13½-15)" [28 (30.5-33-34.5-38)cm] from top of rib, end with RS row facing for next row.

SHAPE FRONT NECK AS FOLLOWS:
Work in patt to last 5 sts, turn (this is neck edge). Leave rem 5 sts on a st holder. Cont in patt, dec 1 st at neck edge on next 9 (10-10-12-15) rows, 25 (27-30-31-34) sts rem. Work even in patt until Left Front measures the same as Back before shoulder shaping, end with RS row facing for next row.

SHAPE SHOULDER AS FOLLOWS:
Cont in patt, BO 8 (9-10-10-11) sts at beg of next row. Work WS row even.

Rep last 2 rows. BO rem 9 (9-10-11-12) sts.

## Sleeve (Make 2)

Using size 6 [4mm] needles and M/C, cast on 42 (48-48-54-54) sts. Work 6 rows in rib as given for Back.

Then beg with a knit row, work in St st throughout, following stripe sequence, *at the same time* inc 1 st at each end of row 5 and every following 6th row 7 (6-12-10-12) times, 58 (62-74-76-80) sts. Then inc 1 st at each end of every 8 (8-4-8-4)th row 4 (5-2-3-4) times, 66 (72-78-82-88) sts.

Work even in patt until Sleeve measures 12½ (13-13½-14-14½)" [32 (33-34.5-35.5-37)cm] from cast-on edge. BO all sts loosely.

## Finishing and Hood

Weave in all ends. Block all pieces to given dimensions.

Join both shoulder seams.

Using size 6 [4mm] needles and M/C, with RS facing beg at Right Front neck, knit across 5 sts from Right Front neck st holder, then pick up and knit 19 (19-19-24-28) sts up Right Front neck, knit across 34 (36-36-40-46) sts from back neck st holder inc 1 st at CB, then pick up and knit 19 (19-19-24-28) sts down Left Front neck, knit across 5 sts from Left Front neck st holder, 83 (85-85-99-113) sts total.

FOLLOWING STRIPE SEQUENCE, WORK IN ST ST WITH GARTER EDGES AS FOLLOWS:
WS rows: K5 in M/C, purl to last 5 sts in strip sequence, k5 in M/C.

RS rows: K5 in M/C, knit to last 5 sts in stripe sequence, k5 in M/C.

Cont in patt as set until Hood measures 6 (6-6-6½-6¾)" [15 (15-15-16.5-17)cm] from pickup row, ending with RS row facing for next row. Place markers either side of center st.

SHAPE TOP OF HOOD AS FOLLOWS:
Cont in patt, work to 2 sts before marker, k2tog, slip marker, k1, slip marker, ssk, work in patt to end.

Cont in patt dec as above on next 17 rows, 47 (49-49-63-77) sts rem.

Divide rem sts evenly onto 2 needles (1 needle will have an extra st). With RS tog BO all sts using the 3-needle bind-off method (work last 2 sts tog on needle with extra st).

WORK FRONT EDGES AS FOLLOWS:
Using size 6 [4mm] needles and M/C, with RS facing, pick up and knit 84 (92-100-104-116) sts up Right Front edge, knit 1 row. BO all sts loosely knitwise.

Rep for Left Front.

Set zipper into CF opening.

Place markers on all four side seams 6 (6½-7-7½-8)" [15 (16.5-18-19-20.5)cm] down from shoulder seams. Sew Sleeves to body between markers.

Sew side and Sleeve seams.

Press lightly, following the instructions on the yarn label.

*red*

The meaning or emotion that each color evokes depends on the culture that you were raised in. Some color associations have similar roots and interpretations but are used symbolically in different ways. White, for example, meaning purity, is used in either marriage or death ceremonies.

Closely linked to fire, red has many associations and symbolic uses. We think of it having lots of energy, so consider it passionate, aggressive, even dangerous. It is used for warning symbols and stoplights. Women of questionable morals are described as being scarlet women, and red letters were used to denounce such behavior in ages past. But in both India and China red is worn by brides to bring good luck. In the practice of feng shui, red is placed carefully for the best use of its high energetic value.

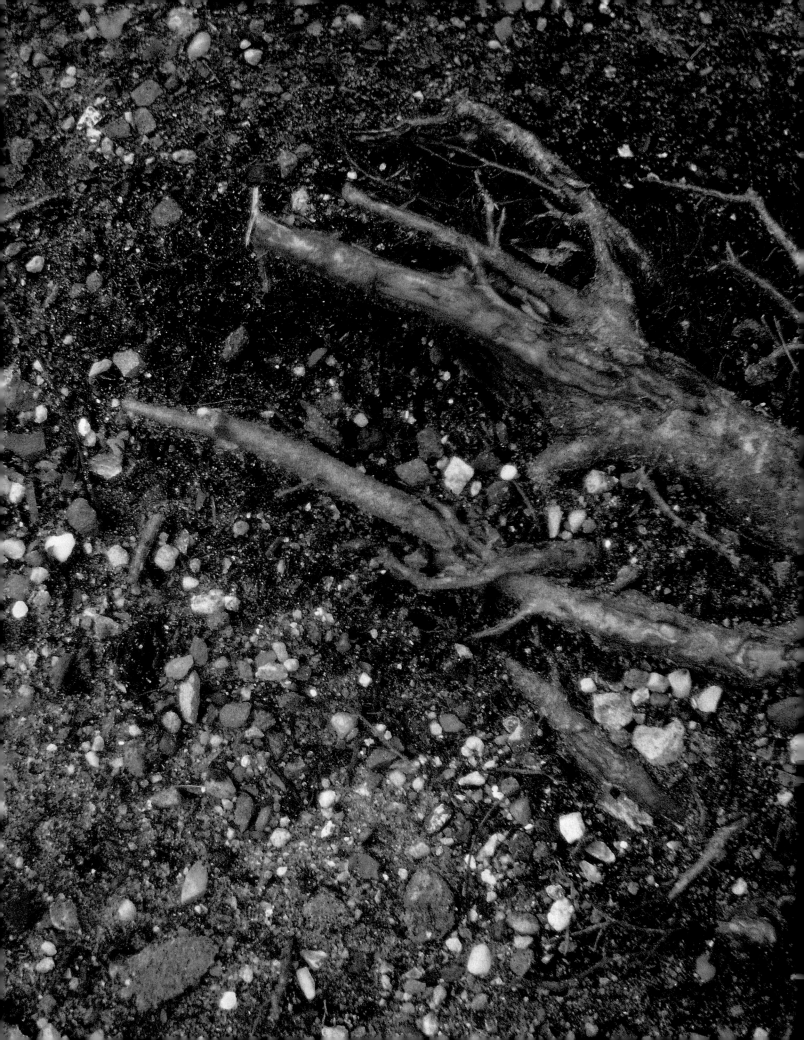

# earth

DARK AND DANK, SCORCHED AND BARREN, green and fertile, valley or mountain—this element has the ability to grow crops and provides the shelter of a cave, but it can be as unstable as it is comforting.

When designing the projects for this chapter, I selected yarns in natural fibers such as wool and hemp to feel rustic and not overly processed. The rich shades of browns, greens, and naturals were inspired by clay and rock. To give a more organic look, the patterning is less symmetrical than those found in traditional Fair Isle garments. The use of felting in some projects further highlights the rustic feel. It also gives the knitter working in Fair Isle patterning for the first time a chance to experiment with the technique, knowing that any discrepancies will "come out in the wash." The projects draw from classic favorites but are updated in their styling.

# peat

## MEN'S RAGLAN SWEATER

All four elements become connected through trees; rooted in earth, they drink up energy from both water and sun as they dance and sway in the wind. They are a source of protection—providing us with shade from the sun, shelter from rain, and a windbreak against the force of strong gusts. They guard us even when we sever their connection to the earth and fashion them into planks or logs to build homes.

Rugged and masculine, this crew-neck sweater incorporates a choppy textured stitch for the body with organically patterned Fair Isle sleeves. This Fair Isle pattern was devised by interpreting the arrangement of the peaks and troughs in the bark of trees.

### Sizes/Finished Chest Measurements

S 44" [112cm]

M 46" [117cm]

L 51" [129.5cm]

XL 56" [142cm]

Instructions are given for the smallest size. If changes are necessary for larger sizes, the instructions are given in ( ). Where there is only one set of figures, this applies to all sizes.

### Materials

M/C, Tussock by Naturally (85% wool, 15% polyester; 203yds [185m]/100g ball) shade 264: 6 (6-7-8) balls

Color A, Naturelle DK by Naturally (100% wool; 210yds [192m]/100g ball) shade 521: 2 (2-2-3) balls

Pair each of size 7 [4.5mm] needles and size 8 [5mm] needles, 4 stitch holders

Yarn amounts given are based on average requirements and are approximate.

### Gauge

22 sts and 22 rows = 4" [10cm] over Fair Isle patt on size 8 [5mm] needles

20 sts and 26 rows = 4" [10cm] over textured patt on size 7 [4.5mm] needles

Take the time to check your gauge; change the needle size if necessary to obtain the correct gauge and garment size.

REFER TO GLOSSARY ON PAGE 23 FOR: **Seed Stitch**

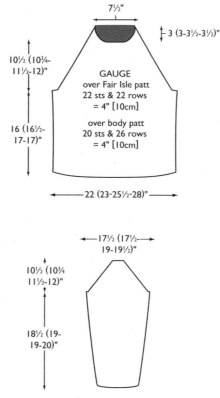

7½"

3 (3-3½-3½)"

10½ (10¾-11½-12)"

GAUGE
over Fair Isle patt
22 sts & 22 rows
= 4" [10cm]

over body patt
20 sts & 26 rows
= 4" [10cm]

16 (16½-17-17)"

22 (23-25½-28)"

17½ (17½-19-19½)"

10½ (10¾-11½-12)"

18½ (19-19-20)"

10½"

L TO R: PEAT RAGLAN SWEATER, GLEN CARDIGAN (SEE PAGE 108).

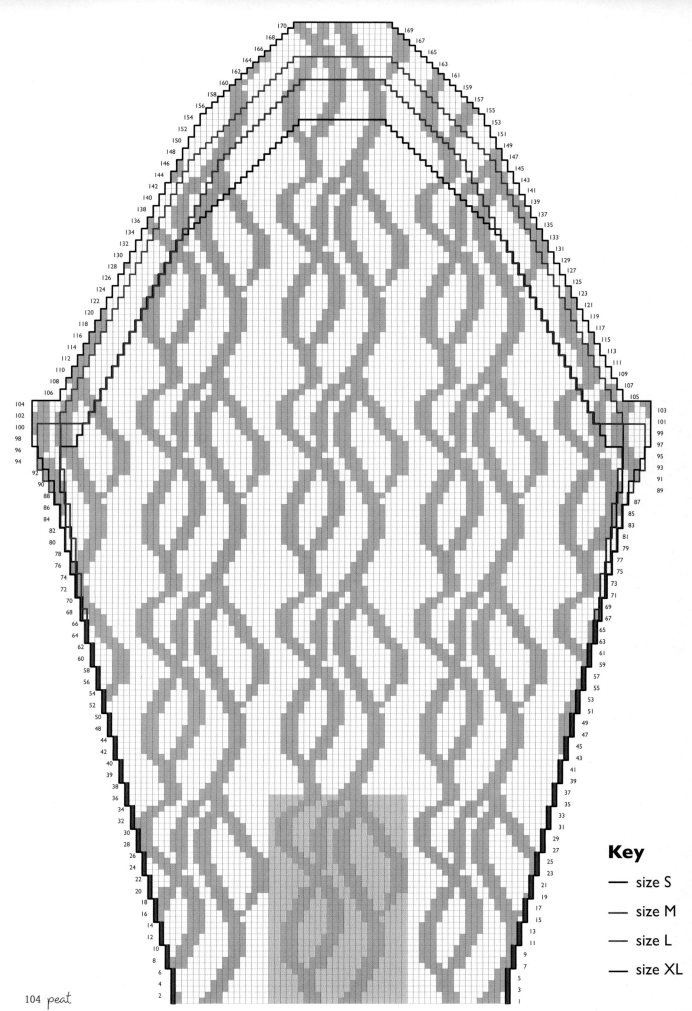

**Key**

— size S

— size M

— size L

— size XL

104 peat

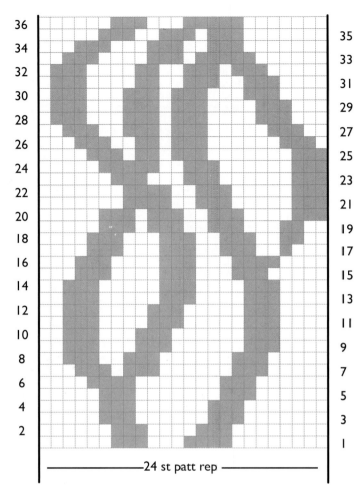

Row numbers on left: 36, 34, 32, 30, 28, 26, 24, 22, 20, 18, 16, 14, 12, 10, 8, 6, 4, 2

Row numbers on right: 35, 33, 31, 29, 27, 25, 23, 21, 19, 17, 15, 13, 11, 9, 7, 5, 3, 1

24 st patt rep

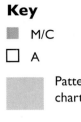

**Key**

■ M/C

□ A

Pattern repeat from chart on page 104.

Chart reads from R to L on RS rows, and from L to R on WS rows.

## Textured Pattern
### (6 St Patt Rep, Plus 2 Sts)

Row 1(WS): P2, *k4, p2; rep from * to end.

Row 2: K2, *p4, k2; rep from * to end.

Rows 3 and 4: Rep Rows 1 and 2.

Row 5: K3, p2, *k4, p2; rep from * to last 3 sts, k3.

Row 6: P3, k2, *p4, k2; rep from * to last 3 sts, p3.

Rows 7 and 8: Rep Rows 5 and 6.

Rep Rows 1–8 for patt.

## Back

Using size 7 [4.5mm] needles and M/C, cast on 110 (116-128-140) sts. Work 1 row in seed st.

Work in Textured Pattern until back measures 16 (16½-17-17)" [40.5 (42-43-43)cm], end with RS row facing for next row.

SHAPE RAGLANS AS FOLLOWS:
Cont in patt, BO 3 (5-4-5) sts at beg of next 2 rows. Then dec 1 st at each end of next 0 (0-10-16) rows, 104 (106-100-98) sts rem. Now dec 1 st at each end of following RS rows 33 (34-31-30) times, 38 sts rem. Work WS row even in patt. Place these sts on a stitch holder.

## Front

Work as given for Back until 58 (58-62-62) sts rem during raglan shaping, end with RS row facing for next row.

SHAPE FRONT NECK AS FOLLOWS:
RS row: Cont in patt, work 2 sts tog, patt across following 20 (20-22-22) sts, turn (this is neck edge). Leave rem 36 (36-38-38) sts on a spare needle.

Working on the 21 (21-23-23) sts only, dec 1 st at neck edge on the next 6 rows, *at the same time* dec 1 st at raglan edge on RS rows only, 12 (12-14-14) sts rem.

Now dec 1 st at neck edge on RS rows (only) 5 times, *at the same time* cont dec 1 st at raglan edge on RS rows, end with WS row facing for next row, 2 (2-4-4) sts rem.

S and M sizes only: Work WS row even. P2tog, break off yarn and draw through last st.

L and XL sizes only: Keeping neck edge even, cont to dec 1 st at raglan edge on next 2 RS rows. Work WS row even. P2tog, break off yarn and draw through last st.

Return to sts on spare needle, slip center 14 sts onto a stitch holder, rejoin yarn, work in patt to last 2 sts, work 2 sts tog.

Working on the 21 (21-23-23) sts only, dec 1 st at neck edge on the following 6 rows, *at the same time* dec 1 st at raglan edge on the RS rows only, 12 (12-14-14) sts rem.

Dec 1 st at neck edge on RS rows (only) 5 times, *at the same time* cont

dec 1 st at raglan edge on RS rows, end with WS row facing for next row, 2 (2-4-4) sts rem.

**S and M sizes only:** Work WS row even. P2tog, break off yarn and draw through last st.

**L and XL sizes only:** Keeping neck edge even, cont to dec 1 st at raglan edge on next 2 RS rows. Work WS row even. P2tog, break off yarn and draw through last st.

## Sleeve (Make 2)

Using size 7 [4.5mm] needles and M/C, cast on 57 sts, knit 4 rows.

Change to size 8 [5mm] needles, beg with Row 1 of chart, work in Fair Isle patt following chart rows in sequence, *at the same time* inc 1 st at each end of Row 7 and every following 4th row 16 (14-20-21) times, 91 (87-99-101) sts on needle. Then inc 1 st at each end of every 6th (6th-2nd-2nd) row 3 (5-3-3) times, 97 (97-105-107) sts. (Inc sts are shown on chart.) Work even following chart until Row 96 (100-100-104) has been completed.

SHAPE RAGLAN AS FOLLOWS:
Cont in patt (as shown on chart), BO 3 (5-4-5) sts at beg of next 2 rows. Then dec 1 st at each end of every RS row 18 (22-22-24) times, 55 (43-53-49) sts rem. Then dec 1 st at each end of every row 20 (14-18-16) times, 15 (15-17-17) sts rem. Leave these sts on a stitch holder.

## Finishing and Neckband

Block all pieces to given dimensions. Taking care to ensure correct side of body pieces are facing to RS, join 3 raglan seams leaving back LHS seam open.

With RS facing, using size 7 [4.5mm] needles and M/C, beg at left Sleeve knit across 15 (15-17-17) sts from left Sleeve st holder, pick up and knit 12 (14-14-17) sts down left front neck, knit across 14 sts from front neck st holder, pick up and knit 12 (14-14-17) sts up right front neck, knit across 15 (15-17-17) sts from right Sleeve and then knit across 38 sts from back neck st holder 106 (110-114-120) sts total. Knit 6 rows, BO all sts loosely.

Join rem raglan seam and neckband seam. Sew side and Sleeve seams.

Press lightly, following the instructions on the yarn label.

## rebirth and renewal

Human survival depends on Mother Earth and on all that she provides. It is, therefore, not surprising that the fruits of the earth, particularly trees, became integral to springtime celebrations of ages past. By marrying the yearly rebirth of plants and the long life span of trees to these festivals, people linked themselves to both the concepts of regeneration and of longevity. The ritualistic use of plants in these celebrations may also point to a belief that the constant return to life of the earth somehow requires human intervention in order for it to be meaningful—or to happen at all.

# glen

## CLASSIC CARDIGAN WITH FELTED POCKETS

For fruitful cultivation of the earth and support of vegetation, water has to be abundant. The glens of Scotland have rivers running through them, rain clouds soak the rolling hills of Ireland, and the moors of England are waterlogged and sodden.

The silhouette of this updated simple cardigan includes a contemporary hood and features bands where the colors from the Fair Isle pattern are repeated.

Felting may be unsuitable for whole garments due to its unpredictability, so the felted Fair Isle patterning is limited to the pockets, where the more solid, less elastic fabric this technique produces is desirable. The patterning, which is asymmetrical in placement, evokes an organic feeling, reminiscent of sprouting plant material.

## Sizes/Finished Chest Measurements

XS 35" [89cm]

S 38" [96.5cm]

M 42" [106.5cm]

L 45" [114cm]

XL 48" [122cm]

2X 52" [132cm]

Instructions are given for the smallest size. If changes are necessary for larger sizes, the instructions are given in ( ). Where there is only one set of figures, this applies to all sizes.

## Materials

Classic Wool by Patons (100% wool, 223yds [204m]/100g ball)

M/C, shade DK Natural Mix 00228: 7 (7-9-10-11-12) balls

Color A, shade Chestnut Brown 00231: 1 ball

Color B, shade Leaf Green 00240: 1 ball

Color C, shade Camel 77023: 1 ball

Color D, shade DK Grey Mix 00225: 1 ball

Color E, shade Russet 00206: 1 ball

Pair each of size 7 [4.5mm] needles and size 10 [6mm] needles, size 7 [4.5mm] circular needle (32" [81cm] long) for front edge of hood, size G/6 [4mm] crochet hook, 7 stitch holders, 6 (6-6-6-7-7) buttons

Yarn amounts given are based on average requirements and are approximate.

## Gauge

24 sts and 19 rows = 4" [10cm] over Fair Isle patt on size 10 [6mm] needles

20 sts and 28 rows = 4" [10cm] over St st on size 7 [4.5mm] needles

Take the time to check your gauge; change the needle size if necessary to obtain the correct gauge and garment size.

REFER TO TECHNIQUES ON PAGE 18 FOR: **Felting, Short Rows, Single Crochet, 3-Needle Bind-Off**

L TO R: PEAT RAGLAN SWEATER, (SEE PAGE 102), GLEN CARDIGAN.

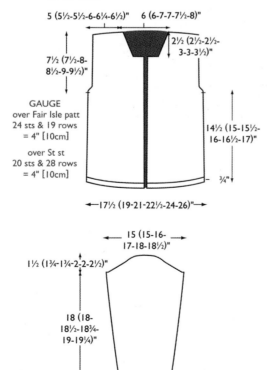

5 (5½-5½-6-6¼-6½)"    6 (6-7-7-7½-8)"

2½ (2½-2½-3-3-3½)"

7½ (7½-8-8½-9-9½)"

GAUGE
over Fair Isle patt
24 sts & 19 rows
= 4" [10cm]

over St st
20 sts & 28 rows
= 4" [10cm]

14½ (15-15½-16-16½-17)"

¾"

←17½ (19-21-22½-24-26)"→

15 (15-16-17-18-18½)"

1½ (1¾-1¾-2-2-2½)"

18 (18-18½-18¾-19-19¼)"

¾"

9½ (9½-10-10-10½-10½)"

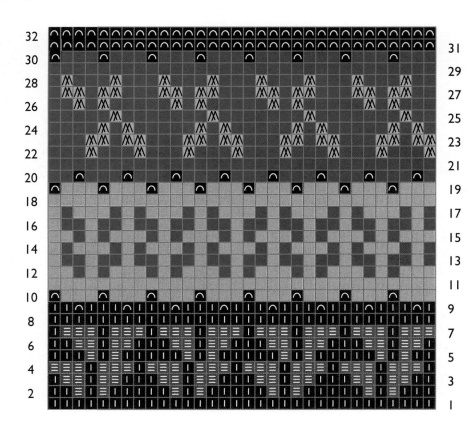

Chart reads from R to L on RS rows, and from L to R on WS rows.

## Back

Using size 7 [4.5mm] needles and Color A, cast on 82 (90-100-104-112-122) sts. Knit 4 rows, inc 6 (6-6-8-8-8) sts evenly across last row, 88 (96-106-112-120-130) sts.

Change to M/C, beg with a knit row, work in St st until Back measures 14½ (15-15½-16-16½-17)" [37 (38-39.5-40.5-42-43)cm], end with RS row facing for next row.

SHAPE ARMHOLES AS FOLLOWS:
Cont in St st, BO 2 (2-3-3-4-5) sts at beg of next 2 rows. Then dec 1 st at each end of next 2 (3-5-6-6-7) rows, 80 (86-90-94-100-106) sts rem.

Work even until armhole measures 7½ (7½-8-8½-9-9½)" [19 (19-20.5-21.5-23-24)cm] from beg of shaping, end with WS row facing for next row.

SHAPE SHOULDERS, WORKING IN SHORT ROWS, AS FOLLOWS:
Next 2 rows: Work to last 9 (10-10-10-11-11) sts, wrap next st, turn, leave rem 9 (10-10-10-11-11) sts unworked.

Next 2 rows: Work to last 17 (19-19-20-21-22) sts, wrap next st, turn, leave rem sts unworked.

Next 2 rows: Work to last 25 (28-28-30-31-33) sts, wrap next st, turn, leave rem sts unworked.

Work across each set of 25 (28-28-30-31-33) sts for shoulder, working wraps tog with the st they wrap. Place each set of sts for shoulder onto separate stitch holders, and rem 30 (30-34-34-38-40) for back neck on a third stitch holder.

## Right Front

Using size 7 [4.5mm] needles and Color A, cast on 39 (43-47-50-54-58) sts. Knit 4 rows, inc 3 (3-3-4-4-4) sts evenly across last row, 42 (46-50-54-58-62) sts.

Change to M/C, beg with a knit row, work in St st until Front measures 14½ (15-15½-16-16½-17)" [37 (38-39-40.5-42-43)cm], end with WS row facing for next row.

SHAPE ARMHOLE AS FOLLOWS:
Cont in St st, BO 2 (2-3-3-4-5) sts at beg of next row (this is armhole edge), purl to end. Then dec 1 st at armhole edge on following 2 (3-5-6-6-7) rows, 38 (41-42-45-48-50) sts rem.

Work even until armhole measures 5 (5-5½-5½-6-6)" [12.5 (12.5-14-14-15-15)cm] from beg of shaping, end with WS row facing for next row.

SHAPE FRONT NECK AS FOLLOWS:
WS row: Purl to last 3 (3-4-5-5-5) sts, turn (this is neck edge), slip rem 3 (3-4-5-5-5) sts onto a stitch holder.

Dec 1 st at neck edge on following 10 (10-10-10-12-12) rows, 25 (28-28-30-31-33) sts rem. Work even until Front measures the same as Back before shoulder shaping, end with RS row facing for next row.

SHAPE SHOULDER, WORKING IN SHORT ROWS, AS FOLLOWS:
RS row: Knit to last 9 (10-10-10-11-11) sts, wrap next st, turn, leave rem 9 (10-10-10-11-11) sts unworked in hold.

Work WS row even.

Next RS row: Work to last 17 (19-19-20-21-22) sts, wrap next st, turn, leave rem sts unworked in hold.

Work WS row even.

Work across these 25 (28-28-28-30-31-33) sts, working wraps tog with the st they wrap. Place sts onto a stitch holder for RH shoulder.

## Left Front

Work as Right Front to armhole shaping, end with RS row facing for next row.

SHAPE ARMHOLE AS FOLLOWS:
Cont in St st, BO 2 (2-3-3-4-5) sts at beg of next row (this is armhole edge), knit to end. Then dec 1 st at armhole edge on following 2 (3-5-6-6-7) rows, 38 (41-42-45-48-50) sts rem.

Work even until armhole measures 5 (5-5½-5½-6-6)" [12.5 (12.5-14-14-15-15)cm] from beg of shaping, end with RS row facing for next row.

SHAPE FRONT NECK AS FOLLOWS:
RS row: Knit to last 3 (3-4-5-5-5) sts, turn (this is neck edge) slip rem 3 (3-4-5-5-5) sts onto a stitch holder.

Dec 1 st at neck edge on following 10 (10-10-10-12-12) rows, 25 (28-28-30-31-33) sts rem. Work even until Front measures the same as Back before shoulder shaping, end with WS row facing for next row.

SHAPE SHOULDER, WORKING IN SHORT ROWS, AS FOLLOWS:
WS row: Purl to last 9 (10-10-10-11-11) sts, wrap next st, turn, leave rem 9 (10-10-10-11-11) sts unworked in hold.

Work RS row even.

Next WS row: Work to last 17 (19-19-19-20-21-22) sts, wrap next st, turn, leave rem sts unworked in hold.

Work RS row even.

Work across these 25 (28-28-30-31-33) sts, working wraps tog with the st they wrap. Place sts onto a stitch holder for LH shoulder.

## Sleeve (Make 2)

Using size 7 [4.5mm] needles and Color A, cast on 44 (44-46-46-48-48) sts, knit 4 rows, inc 4 sts evenly across last row, 48 (48-50-50-52-52) sts.

Change to M/C, beg with a knit row work in St st inc 1 st at each end of row 5 and every following 8th row 12 (12-14-10-5-3) times, 74 (74-80-72-64-60) sts. Then inc 1 st at each end of every 10 (10-0-6-6-6)th row 1 (1-0-6-13-16) time, 76 (76-80-84-90-92) sts. Work even in St st until Sleeve measures 18 (18-18½-18¾-19-19¼)" [45.5 (45.5-47-47.5-48.5-49)cm] from cast-on edge, end with RS row facing for next row.

SHAPE SLEEVE CAP FOLLOWS:
Cont in St st, BO 5 (4-6-4-6-5) sts at beg of next 2 rows. Then BO 6 (5-5-5-5-4) sts at beg of following 8 (10-10-12-12-16) rows. BO rem 18 (18-18-16-18-18) sts loosely.

## Pockets

Using size 10 [6mm] needles and Color A, cast on 28 sts, knit 2 rows, inc 4 sts evenly across 2nd row, 32 sts. Working in St st, beg with a knit row work Rows 1–32 from chart, changing colors as indicated.

Using Color A, knit 2 rows, dec 4 sts across last row. BO all sts.

Using size 10 [6mm] needles and Color A, with RS of Pocket facing, pick up and knit 28 along each side edge of Pocket, purl 2 rows. BO all sts.

## Finishing and Hood

Weave in all ends. Block all pieces to given dimensions.

Using size 7 [4.5mm] needles and M/C, join both shoulder seams by the 3-needle bind-off method, working with WS together so that the seams show on the RS of garment.

WORK RHS HOOD AS FOLLOWS:
Using size 7 [4.5mm] needles and M/C, beg at RHS of CF with RS facing, knit across 3 (3-4-5-5-5) sts from front neck stitch holder, then pick up and knit 24 (24-24-28-28-32) sts up Right Front neck, work across 15 (15-17-17-19-20) sts from back neck stitch holder. Leave rem 15 (15-17-17-19-20) sts on back neck stitch holder for LHS hood. Working on the 42 (42-45-50-52-57) sts, beg with a purl row, work in St st until Hood measures 9 (9-9-9.5-9.5-10)" [23 (23-23-24-24-25.5)cm] from pick-up row, ending with a WS row facing for next row.

SHAPE TOP OF HOOD AS FOLLOWS:
Dec 1 st at beg of next row. Dec 1 st at end of following row. BO 2 sts at beg of next row. Work RS row even. BO 4 sts at beg of next row. Work RS row even. BO 6 sts at beg of next row. Work RS row even. BO 9 (9-10-12-12-13) sts at beg of next row. Work RS row even. Rep last 2 rows once more. BO rem 10 (10-11-12-14-17) sts.

WORK LHS HOOD AS FOLLOWS:
Using size 7 [4.5mm] needle and M/C, beg at center of sts on back neck stitch holder, with RS facing, knit across 15 (15-17-17-19-20) sts from back neck stitch holder, then pick up and knit 24 (24-24-28-28-32) sts down Left Front neck and knit across 3 (3-4-5-5-5) sts from front neck stitch holder. Working on the 42 (42-45-50-52-57) sts, beg with a purl row, work in St st until Hood measures 9 (9-9-9½-9½-10)" [23 (23-23-24-24-25.5)cm] from pickup row, ending with RS row facing for next row.

SHAPE TOP OF HOOD AS FOLLOWS:
Dec 1 st at beg of next row. Dec 1 st at end of following row. BO 2 sts at beg of next row. Work WS row even. BO 4 sts at beg of next row. Work WS row even. BO 6 sts at beg of next row. Work WS row even. BO 9 (9-10-12-12-13) sts at beg of next row. Work WS row even. Rep last 2 rows once more. BO rem 10 (10-11-12-14-17) sts.

WORK LEFT FRONT BAND AS FOLLOWS:
Using size 7 [4.5mm] needles and M/C, with RS facing pick up and knit 100 (100-108-120-128-128) sts down left side of CF ending at top of contrast garter edge at lower edge. Knit 1 row.

Work in Fair Isle patt following Rows 9 and 10 of chart, changing colors as

indicated. Change to Color E, knit 2 rows, Change to Color B, knit 2 rows, dec 6 (6-6-8-10-10) sts evenly across last row, 94 (94-102-112-118-118) sts rem. BO all sts loosely.

### WORK RIGHT FRONT BAND AS FOLLOWS:

Using size 7 [4.5mm] needles and M/C, with RS facing, pick up and knit 100 (100-108-120-128-128) sts up right side of CF beg at top of contrast garter edge at lower edge. Knit 1 row.

Work in Fair Isle patt following Rows 9 and 10 of chart, changing colors as indicated. Change to Color E, knit 1 row.

### WORK BUTTONHOLE ROW AS FOLLOWS:

K4 (4-2-4-2-2), *k2tog, (YO) twice, k2tog, k14 (14-16-18-16-16); rep from * 4 (4-4-4-5-5) more times, k2tog, (YO), twice, k2tog, k2.

Change to Color B, knit 2 rows, dec 6 (6-6-8-10-10) sts evenly across last row, 94 (94-102-112-118-118) sts rem. BO all sts loosely.

### SET IN SLEEVES TO ARMHOLES AS FOLLOWS:

Using size 7 [4.5mm] needles and M/C, pick up and knit 100 (100-106-112-118-124) sts along top edge of Sleeve. Using size 7 [4.5mm] needles and M/C, pick up and knit 100 (100-106-112-118-124) sts around arm-hole. Join Sleeves to body by the 3-needle bind-off method, working with WS of garment tog so that seams show on the RS of garment.

Sew side and Sleeve seams. Sew center back seam on Hood.

### WORK HOOD EDGING AS FOLLOWS:

Using circular size 7 [4.5mm] needle and Color A, with RS facing and beg at edge of right front band, pick up and knit 4 sts along right front band,

132 sts around front edge of Hood, then pick up and knit 4 sts across top of left front band, 140 sts. Knit 3 rows. BO all sts knitwise.

Using Color A and crochet hook, neaten lower edge of front bands by working single crochet across bottom of both bands.

Felt Pockets, basting them tog with sewing thread before washing so that they remain the same size after shrinking.

Place marker 6½" [16.5cm] from CF band and 1½" [4cm] from lower edge to indicate bottom corner of Pocket. Sew on Pocket placing at an approx 30-degree angle. Rep for second Pocket.

Sew buttons onto Left Front Band to match buttonholes.

Press lightly, following the instructions on the yarn label.

# the festival of lammas

Lammas, celebrated on the first of August, was originally a festival to celebrate the first crop of the summer. Thanks were given for the earth's bounty by blessing bread made from the first grains of the season. We still vaguely celebrate Lammas by having strawberry or asparagus festivals and through farmers' markets, where local produce is sold. In these days of having many foods available to us year-round, we still welcome the enjoyment of a meal comprising the first corn, new potatoes, berries, and other produce that tending the local soil brings to us.

# petroglyph PILLOW

The people of ancient civilizations made art using the natural materials found around them. Sticks, small rocks, or plant materials were used as their paint, the land and the walls of caves as their canvas. Rock carvings are a source of fascination for many of us: Why did people from these times draw images into the Earth's surface? Do these images have meaning or are they simply a forerunner of our graffiti art?

Drawing its inspiration from the stylized images found in the petroglyphs of North America, this pillow is made in an earthy, organic-feeling hemp-blend yarn. Its colors are reminiscent of the hues of rocks found throughout this world; the stripes mirror the layers built up over many ages.

## Finished Measurements

Pillow is 16" [40.5cm] square.

## Materials

Hempwol by Lanaknits Designs (50% hemp, 50% wool; 254yds [240m]/100g skein).

1 skein each in the following shades:

Color A, Natural

Color B, Pecan

Color C, Silver Sage

Color D, Peridot

Color E, Sunflower

Color F, Aubergine

Pair each of size 6 [4mm] needles and size 7 [4.5mm] needles, plus 1 extra size 6 [4mm] needle for 3-needle bind-off, blunt large-eyed needle for duplicate stitch, 16" [40.5cm] square pillow form

## Gauge

24 sts and 24 rows = 4" [10cm] over Fair Isle patt on size 7 [4.5mm] needles

22 sts and 30 rows = 4" [10cm] over St st on size 6 [4mm] needles

Take the time to check your gauge; change the needle size if necessary to obtain the correct gauge.

TO TECHNIQUES ON PAGE 18 FOR: **Duplicate Stitch, 3-Needle Bind Off**

REFER TO GLOSSARY ON PAGE 23 FOR: **Seed Stitch, Garter Ridge**

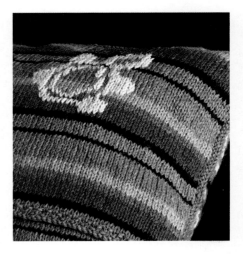

## Placement of Chart Patterns

| Chart B | Chart C | Chart A | Chart E |
|---------|---------|---------|---------|
| Chart F | Chart B | Chart E | Chart D |
| Chart E | Chart A | Chart D | Chart C |
| Chart D | Chart C | Chart B | Chart A |

## Chart A

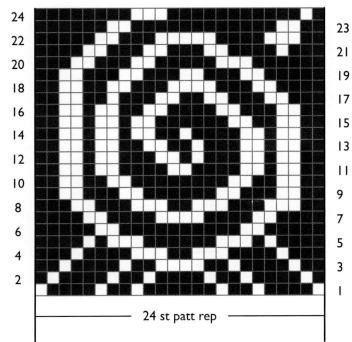

24 st patt rep

**Key**

■ Background; see stripe sequence

□ A

Chart reads from R to L
on RS rows, and from
L to R on WS rows.

## Chart B

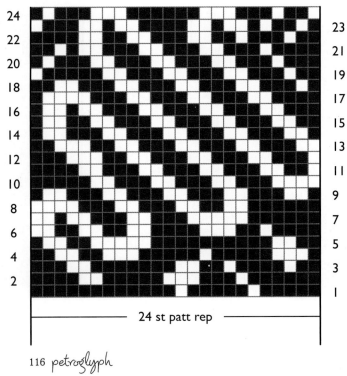

24 st patt rep

**Key**

■ Background; see stripe sequence

□ A

Chart reads from R to L
on RS rows, and from
L to R on WS rows.

## Chart C

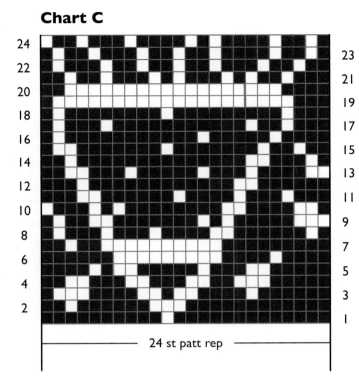

24 st patt rep

**Key**

■ Background; see stripe sequence

☐ A

Chart reads from R to L
on RS rows, and from
L to R on WS rows.

## Chart D

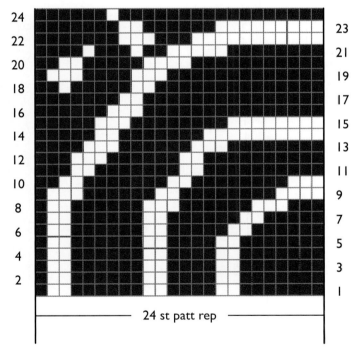

24 st patt rep

**Key**

■ Background; see stripe sequence

☐ A

Chart reads from R to L
on RS rows, and from
L to R on WS rows.

## Chart E

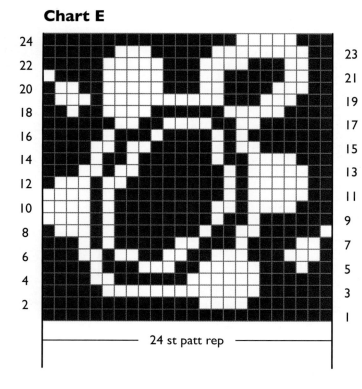

24  
22  
20  
18  
16  
14  
12  
10  
8  
6  
4  
2  

23  
21  
19  
17  
15  
13  
11  
9  
7  
5  
3  
1  

— 24 st patt rep —

### Key

■ Background; see stripe sequence

□ A

Chart reads from R to L  
on RS rows, and from  
L to R on WS rows.

## Chart F

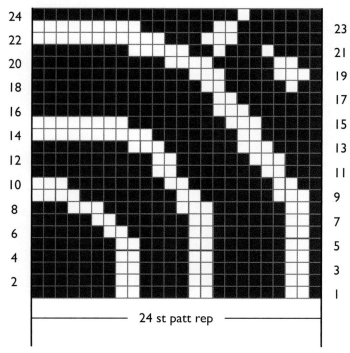

24  
22  
20  
18  
16  
14  
12  
10  
8  
6  
4  
2  

23  
21  
19  
17  
15  
13  
11  
9  
7  
5  
3  
1  

— 24 st patt rep —

### Key

■ Background; see stripe sequence

□ A

Chart reads from R to L  
on RS rows, and from  
L to R on WS rows.

## Stripe Sequence

2 rows in Color B

3 rows in Color C

2 rows in Color D

5 rows in Color E

2 rows in Color F

4 rows in Color B

1 row in Color F

5 rows in Color B

## Pillow

Beginning at CB of pillow, using size 6 [4mm] needles and Color B, cast on 88 sts. Work 2 rows in seed st.

Then, working in St st, beg with a knit row, work 72 rows in stripe sequence (3 reps of stripe sequence). Using Color B, knit 2 rows (garter ridge), inc 8 sts evenly across last row, 96 sts.

Change to size 7 [4.5mm] needles, cont in stripe sequence for background colors, work in Fair Isle patt, placing each chart as given in diagram (96 rows total).

Change back to size 6 [4mm] needles, using Color B knit 2 rows (2nd garter ridge), dec 8 sts evenly across last row, 88 sts.

Now, working in St st, beg with a knit row, work stripe sequence over next 72 rows. Using Color B, work 2 rows in seed st. BO all sts.

Fold last 72 rows at the 2nd garter ridge to form upper part of back. Place marker 4" [10cm] in from RH edge and 6" [15cm] down from fold to indicate bottom RH side of chart. This point will be st 1, Row 1 of chart. Using Color A, following Chart E, work chart in duplicate st.

Sew in all ends. Block out piece to given dimensions.

Fold first set of 72 rows at the 1st garter edge to form lower part of back, tucking under the upper part where they overlap.

JOIN LHS SEAM AS FOLLOWS:
**Using size 6 [4mm] needles and Color B, with RS facing, pick up 96 sts along LHS front of Pillow. Using another size 6 [4mm] needle and Color B, with RS facing, pick up and knit 96 sts along LHS back of Pillow, working through both layers where the 2 parts overlap.

Using 3-needle bind-off method, with WS tog so seam is on the RS of pillow, BO all sts.

Rep from ** to ** for RHS seam.

Press lightly, following the instructions on the yarn label. Place pillow form in Pillow.

## painting on the earth

Some of the earliest recorded paintings in the world are the cave paintings in Lascaux, France, believed to date from 15,000 BC. These were made with pigments made from ground red and yellow ocher, found in the local clay, and applied to the cave walls using bundles of grasses or reeds. The rock's porous nature allowed the images to sink in and the darkened environment preserved them over the ages.

Using materials provided by the earth has allowed people to create art throughout history. Although today a multitude of paint colors are produced synthetically, we still use many naturally occurring pigments.

# canyon

## FELTED BAG

When we think about the theme "earth," we often think of organic material—rocks, soil, or clay—in varied landscapes. They all share the traits of being substantial, weighty, and dense. Canyons and gorges conjure images of slowly evolving panoramas created as hard, seemingly unyielding rock formations shift or are worn away.

Inspired by the colors of American Southwest landscapes, this felted bag is a great project for a first attempt at Fair Isle knitting. The felting process shrinks the fabric and makes it denser, so any imperfections in the knitting become difficult to detect. Two easy-to-follow patterns were selected to give you the opportunity to work from different charts, reflecting the diversity that can be found even within one specific geological area.

## Finished Measurements

Bag measures 28" [71cm] around and 13" [33cm] deep before felting, and approx 24" [61cm] around and 12" [61cm] deep after felting

## Materials

Classic Wool by Patons (100% wool; 223yds [204m]/100g ball)

1 ball each in the following shades:

M/C, Deep Olive shade 00205

Color A, Rich Red shade 00207

Color B, Paprika shade 00238

Color C, Old Gold shade 00204

Pair of size 10 [6mm] needles, size 10 [6mm] circular needle (16" [40.5cm] long), pair of size 10 [6mm] dpns, 1 button

## Gauge

20 sts and 22 rows = 4" [10cm] over Fair Isle patt on size 10 [6mm] needles before felting.

Take the time to check your gauge; change the needle size if necessary to obtain the correct gauge.

REFER TO TECHNIQUES ON PAGE 18 FOR: **Felting, I-cord, Buttonhole Stitch**

REFER TO GLOSSARY ON PAGE 23 FOR: **Garter Stitch, Garter Ridge**

## Chart A

Chart reads from R to L on RS rows, and from L to R on WS rows.

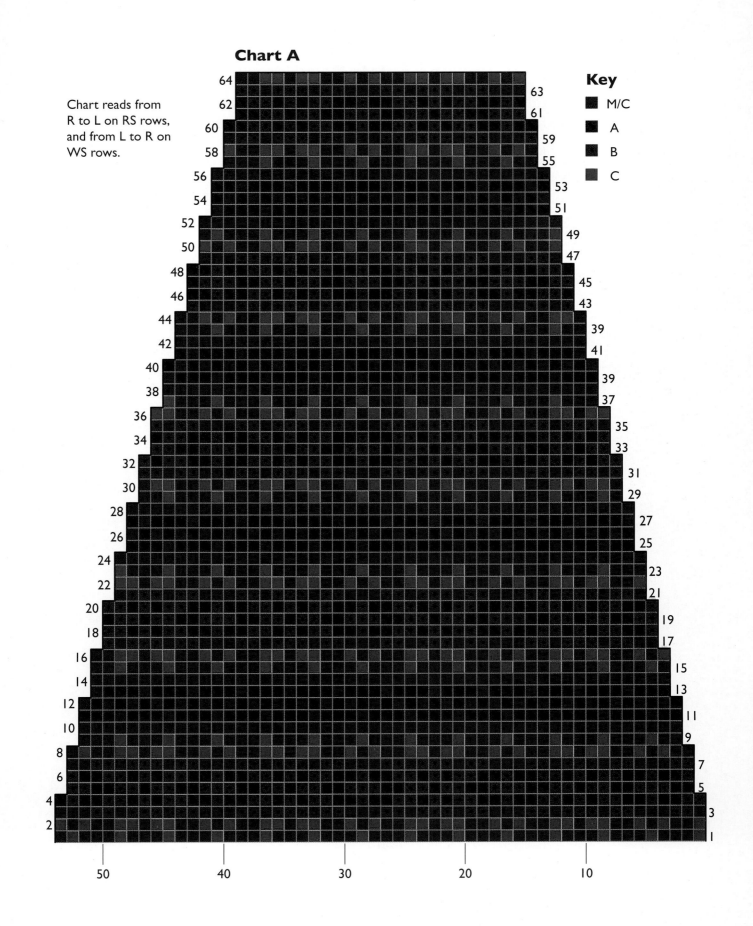

**Key**
- ■ M/C
- ■ A
- ■ B
- ■ C

**Chart B**

Chart reads from R to L on RS rows, and from L to R on WS rows.

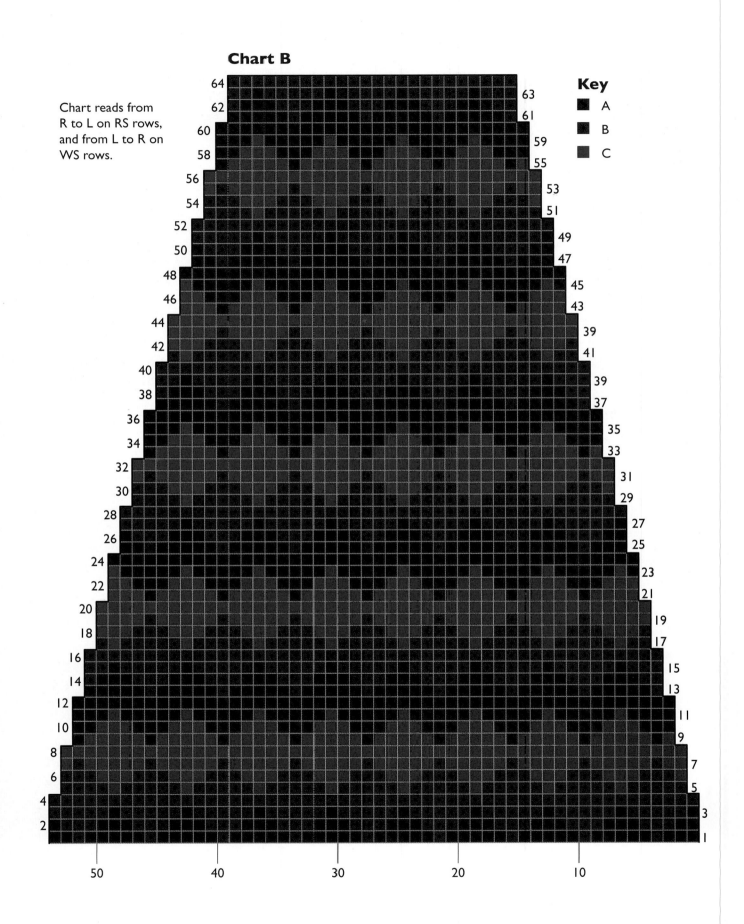

**Key**
- ■ A
- ■ B
- ■ C

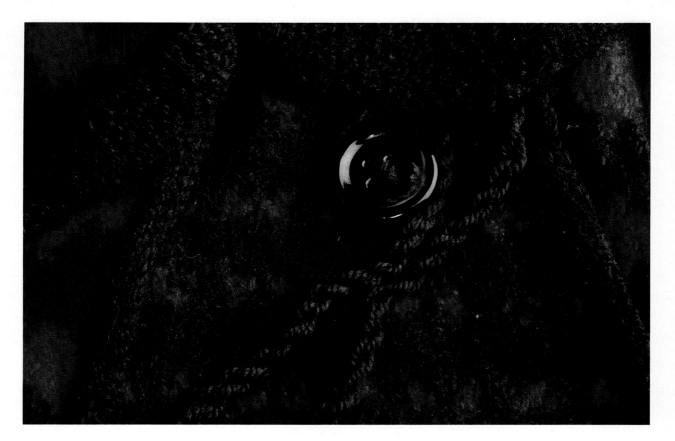

## Front/Back (Make 2)

Using size 10 [6mm] needles and M/C, cast on 54 sts. Knit 1 row (WS).

Beg with a knit row, and following Row 1 of Chart A, work in Fair Isle patt as shown in chart, changing colors as indicated and dec 1 st at each end of Row 5, then every 4th row 14 times as shown, 24 sts rem.

Using M/C, knit 1 row. BO all sts.

## Sides (Make 2)

Using size 10 [6mm] needles and Color B, cast on 54 sts. Knit 1 row (WS).

Beg with a knit row, and following Row 1 of Chart B, work in Fair Isle patt as shown in chart, changing colors as indicated and dec 1 st at each end of Row 5, then every 4th row 14 times as shown, 24 sts rem.

Using Color A, knit 1 row. BO all sts.

## Base

Using size 10 [6mm] needles and M/C, cast on 30 sts, beg with a knit row, work in St st throughout, inc 1 st at each end of row 2 and following 5 rows, 42 sts. Work even for another 4½" [11.5cm]. Then dec 1 st at each end of next 6 rows, 30 sts rem.

BO all sts loosely.

## Straps (Make 2)

Using size 10 [6mm] needles and M/C, cast on 5 sts, work in garter st until strap measures approx 22" [56cm] when stretched slightly. BO all sts.

## Finishing

Sew in ends. Place pieces tog with cast-on edges of both the Front and Back at the bottom and the BO edges of Side pieces also at the bottom.

Sew Base to bottom edge, matching the section worked even to bottom of Sides.

Sew all four seams of bag.

MAKE I-CORDS AS FOLLOWS:
Using size 10 [6mm] dpns and M/C, make four 4 st I-cords 12" [30.5cm] long.

Sew I-cords in place over each of the four seams.

## Drawstring Band

Using size 10 [6mm] circular needle and M/C, pick up 145 sts around top edge of bag. Working in rnds, place marker to indicate beg of rnd. Knit 1 rnd, purl 1 rnd (garter ridge).

WORK EYELET RND AS FOLLOWS:
(K2tog, YO) to last st, k1.

Knit 1 rnd, purl 1 rnd (garter ridge). BO all sts loosely.

## Flap

Place markers on drawstring band pick-up row 1½" [4cm] out from seams on back. Using size 10 [6mm] needles and M/C, pick up and knit 36 sts between markers. Work in garter st for 2" [5cm]. Dec 1 st at each end of next row and following alt rows 11 times, BO rem 12 sts.

Stitch on straps at lower edge where seams meet the base and at the upper edge at edges of flap.

Felt the bag following instructions on page 18. After felting, pull bag into shape and leave to dry.

MAKE DRAWSTRING CORD AS FOLLOWS:
Cut 2 lengths of M/C 95" [241cm] long. With both strands tog, hold one end and, with somebody holding the other end, twist strands to the right until they begin to curl. Fold the 2 ends tog and tie in a knot. The strands will twist themselves tog.

Thread the drawstring through eyelets beg and ending at CF.

Sometimes the eyelets may close up during the felting process, so you may need to poke a knitting needle through them to spread them out again.

Make loop using buttonhole stitch at center point on underside of flap, sew on button to match loop.

# yarn color names

At the beginning of the twentieth century, the colors available in a box of crayons were limited, and their names were the obvious red, blue, green, orange, and so forth. Today, a typical box might include 120 shades, and their names have become both more obscure and specific in order to capture the imagination.

The names of the colors found on a yarn company's shade cards will typically include ones taken from nature. We might find the names of precious stones or trees, florals such as delphinium or geranium, or food references such as mango, pistachio, or the names of spices. These names have always had the ability to draw us or repel us, and because of the latter, some companies steer away from names entirely, using numbers instead.

# tundra

## CLASSIC YOKED SWEATER

Rocky landscapes known as tundra are treeless and barren, yet still display their own kind of craggy earthy beauty. Although little grows there, this part of our world supports many life-forms. Its history and stories are captured in intricate fossils preserved in its rock formations—some of them dating from the Ice Age.

The Fair Isle patterning used here draws its inspiration from these ancient fossil remains. The sophisticated patterns are set in a classic yoke-style sweater—a silhouette that has become synonymous with northern landscapes through Scandinavian or Inuit traditional dress. But this outdoor sweater is lighter in weight and therefore more suitable for layering or for wearing in more hospitable climates than the tundra.

### Sizes / Finished Chest Measurements

S 35½" [90cm]

M 39" [99cm]

L 42½" [108cm]

XL 46" [117cm]

2X 50" [127cm]

3X 53" [134.5cm]

Instructions are given for the smallest size. If changes are necessary for larger sizes, the instructions are given in ( ). Where there is only one set of figures, this applies to all sizes.

### Materials

Morehouse Merino 2-Ply by Morehouse Farm (100% wool; 220yds [201m]/50g skein).

M/C, Natural Soft White: 5 (6-7-8-9-10) skeins

Color A, Natural Brown Heather: 5 (6-7-8-9-10) skeins

Size 6 [4mm] circular needles (32" [81cm] and 16" [40.5cm] long), size 7 [4.5mm] circular needle (32" [81cm] long), set of size 6 [4mm] and size 7 [4.5mm] dpns (for sleeve), 4 st holders

Yarn amounts given are based on average requirements and are approximate.

### Gauge

27 sts and 26 rnds = 4" [10cm] over Fair Isle patt on circular size 6 [4mm] needle.

Take the time to check your gauge; change the needle size if necessary to obtain the correct gauge and garment size.

REFER TO THINGS YOU NEED TO KNOW ON PAGE 14 FOR:
**Working in the Round**

### Note on Increases

M1, work sleeve increase by picking up strand between sts.

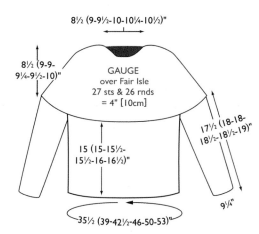

8½ (9-9½-10-10¼-10½)"

8½ (9-9¼-9½-10)"

GAUGE
over Fair Isle
27 sts & 26 rnds
= 4" [10cm]

17½ (18-18-18½-18½-19)"

15 (15-15½-15½-16-16½)"

9¼"

35½ (39-42½-46-50-53)"

## Chart A

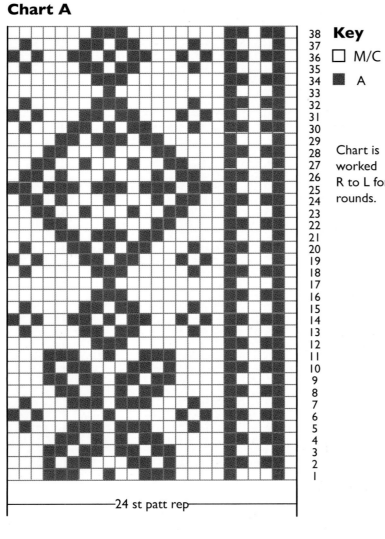

38
37
36
35
34
33
32
31
30
29
28
27
26
25
24
23
22
21
20
19
18
17
16
15
14
13
12
11
10
9
8
7
6
5
4
3
2
1

**Key**

 M/C

■ A

Chart is
worked
R to L for all
rounds.

|—— 24 st patt rep ——|

## Chart B

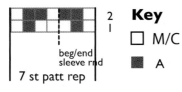

2
1

beg/end
sleeve rnd

7 st patt rep

**Key**

☐ M/C

■ A

Chart is worked
R to L for all rounds.

## Chart D

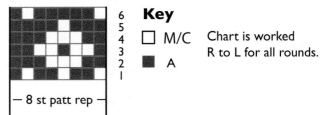

6
5
4
3
2
1

**Key**

☐ M/C

■ A

Chart is worked
R to L for all rounds.

|— 8 st patt rep —|

## Chart C

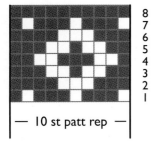

8
7
6
5
4
3
2
1

**Key**

☐ M/C

■ A

Chart is worked
R to L for all rounds.

|— 10 st patt rep —|

## Chart E

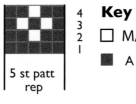

4
3
2
1

**Key**

☐ M/C

■ A

Chart is worked
R to L for all rounds.

5 st patt
rep

## Body

Using longer size 6 [4mm] circular needle and M/C, cast on 220 (244-268-282-306-330) sts. Place marker to indicate beg of round and join, being careful not to twist.

Knit 1 rnd, purl 1 rnd. Rep last 2 rnds once more, inc 20 (20-20-30-30-30) sts evenly on last rnd, 240 (264-288-312-336-360) sts. Change to size 7 [4.5mm] circular needle.

Working in the round, beg with Rnd 1 (1-34-34-32-28) Chart A, work 24 st patt rep 10 (11-12-13-14-15) times. Work chart rnds in sequence until Body measures approx 15 (15-15½-15½-16-16½)" [38 (38-39-39-40.5-42)cm], end by working Rnd 16 Chart A.

### DIVIDE FOR FRONT AND BACK AS FOLLOWS:

Change to Color A and knit 1 rnd ending 10 (10-12-12-12-12) sts before marker, BO 20 (20-24-24-24-24) sts, knit 100 (112-120-132-144-156) sts, BO 20 (20-24-24-24-24) sts, knit to end. Place each set of 100 (112-120-132-144-156) sts onto separate stitch holders for Front and Back.

## Sleeve (Make 2)

Using size 6 [4mm] dpns and M/C, cast on 54 sts. Place marker to indicate beg of round and join, being careful not to twist. Divide sts evenly between 3 needles.

Knit 1 rnd, purl 1 rnd. Rep these 2 rnds once more, inc 8 sts evenly on last rnd, 62 sts. Change to size 7 [4.5mm] dpns.

Working in the round, beg with Rnd 1 Chart B and Rnd 19 (17-17-13-13-11) Chart A, work last 4 sts as shown at LHS Chart B once, then work 24 st patt rep Chart A twice, then work 7 st patt rep Chart B once, followed by first 3 sts shown at RHS Chart B once. Cont working chart rnds in sequence as set until 4 rnds have been completed.

**Next rnd:** Work 1 st, m1 (see note page 15), work in patt as set to last st before marker, m1, work last st.

Cont inc 1 st each side of marker in this way every 6th rnd 15 (13-9-6-4-2) more times, 94 (90-82-76-72-68) sts. Then inc 1 st each side of marker every 4th rnd 3 (7-13-18-21-25) times, 100 (104-108-112-114-118) sts. Work all inc sts following Chart B.

Work even until Sleeve measures approx 17½ (18-18-18½-18½-19)" [44.5 (45.5-45.5-47-47-48.5)cm] from cast-on edge end by working Rnd 16 Chart A.

Change to Color A and knit 1 rnd ending last rnd 10 (10-12-12-12-12) sts before marker.

**Next rnd:** BO 20 (20-24-24-24-24) sts, knit to end.

Leave rem 80 (84-84-88-90-94) sts on a stitch holder.

## Yoke

Using size 7 [4.5mm] circular needle and Color A, p80 (84-84-88-90-94) sts from left sleeve, p100 (112-120-132-144-156) sts from front, p80 (84-84-88-90-94) sts from right sleeve, p100 (112-120-132-144-156) sts from back and join into a rnd, 360 (392-408-440-468-500) sts total. Knit 1 rnd. Purl 1 rnd.

**Next rnd:** Knit, dec 0 (2-8-10-8-10) sts evenly across rnd, 360 (390-400-430-460-490) sts rem. Place markers to designate 10 st patt rep and for decreasing evenly on next rnd.

**Next rnd:** Following Rnd 1 Chart C work 10 st patt rep 36 (39-40-43-46-49) times across rnd.

Work Rnds 2–8 Chart C in sequence.

**Dec rnd:** Using Color A, *p8, p2tog; rep from * to end, 324 (351-360-387-414-441) sts rem.

Using Color A, knit 1 rnd, purl 1 rnd.

**Dec rnd:** Using Color A, *k7, k2tog; work from * to end, 288 (312-320-344-368-392) sts rem.

Using Color A, purl 1 rnd, knit 1 rnd, purl 1 rnd.

**Next rnd:** Following Rnd 1 Chart D, work 8 st patt rep 36 (39-40-43-46-49) times across rnd.

Work Rnds 2–6 Chart D in sequence.

**Dec rnd:** Using Color A, *k6, k2tog; rep from * to end, 252 (273-280-301-322-343) sts rem.

Using Color A, purl 1 rnd, knit 1 rnd, purl 1 rnd (27 rnds worked on Yoke).

**Dec rnd:** Using Color A, *k5, k2tog; rep from * to end, 216 (234-240-258-276-294) sts rem.

Purl 1 rnd.

**Dec rnd:** Using Color A, *k4, k2tog; rep from * to end, 180 (195-200-215-230-245) sts rem.

**Next rnd:** Following Rnd 1 Chart E, work 5 st patt rep 36 (39-40-43-46-49) times across rnd.

Work Rnds 2–4 Chart E in sequence.

**Dec rnd:** Using Color A, *k3, k2tog; rep from * to end, 144 (156-160-172-184-196) sts rem.

Knit 1 rnd (37 rnds worked on Yoke).

**Dec rnd:** Purl, dec 18 (20-20-26-32-40) sts evenly across rnd, 126 (136-140-146-152-156) sts rem.

Knit 1 rnd, purl 1 rnd (40 rnds worked on Yoke).

Change to shorter size 6 [4mm] needle. Using Color A throughout and knitting all rnds, work 14 (18-18-20-22-24) more rnds. Place marker to indicate rnd for pick-up for second neckline.

### WORK NECKBAND AS FOLLOWS:

Using Color A, dec 12 sts evenly across next rnd, 114 (124-128-134-140-144) sts rem.

Work in seed st as follows:

**Next rnd:** (K1, p1) to end.

**Next rnd:** (P1, k1) to end.

Rep the last 2 rnds once more.

Knit 1 rnd. Purl 1 rnd. Rep the last 2 rnds twice more. BO all sts loosely using size 7 [4.5mm] needle.

**WORK SECOND NECKLINE AS FOLLOWS:**
Using shorter size 6 [4mm] needle and M/C, working on WS of garment, pick up and knit 114 (124-128-134-140-144) sts evenly around rnd indicated by marker.

Knit 6 rnds. Work 2 rnds in seed st as before. Knit 8 rnds. BO all sts loosely using size 7 [4.5mm] needle. Allow last 8 rnds to roll down and sew to seed st rnds at sides of neck.

## Finishing

Weave in all ends. Block garment to given dimensions. Join armholes below Yoke.

Press lightly, following the instructions given on the yarn label.

# aristotle and the elements

Aristotle believed that the "simple bodies" of fire, air, water, and earth were each made from two of the "elements" of hot, cold, moist, and dry. He also thought that the simple bodies could change into each another by exchanging one of their component elements—fire (dry and hot) could change into air (moist and hot) by exchanging the dry for moist. Similarly, air could exchange its hot for cold to become water. He depicted this theory of behavior as a pattern of change, where each simple body could change into another until the process came full circle.

# guide to projects and yarns used

## water

NAUTICAL
(page 26)
 Young Touch Cotton DK by Estelle Designs (100% merceized cotton: 114yds [105m]/50g ball)

WAVES
(page 30)
 Extra by Needful Yarns (100% merino wool; 99yds [90 m]/50g ball)

SPINDRIFT
(page 34)
 Cotton Twist by Berroco (70% mercerized cotton, 30% rayon; 85yds [78m]/50g skein)

Mirror FX by Berroco (100% polyester; 60yds (55m)/10g ball)

CRYSTAL
(page 38)
Merino/Alpaca by SweaterKits (60% merino, 40% alpaca; 120yds [110m]/50g ball)

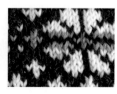

OCEAN
(page 44)
18/24 Wool by Mission Falls (100% wool; 85yds [78m]/50g ball)

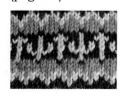

## air

SWAY
(page 52)
 Anti-Tickle Merino Blend DK by King Cole (100% superwash wool; 123yds [112m]/50g ball)

DRIFTING
(page 58)
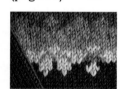 Anti-Tickle Merino Blend DK by King Cole (100% superwash wool; 123yds [112m]/50g ball)

BREEZE
(page 62)
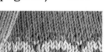 Basics-Stop by Lana Grossa (50% viscose, 50% microfiber; 115yds [105m]/50g ball)

SWIRL
(page 66)
La Gran by Classic Elite (76.5% mohair, 17.5% wool, 6% nylon; 90yds [82m]/42g ball)

WHISPER
(page 71)
Angorissima by Diamond (100% angora; 123yds [114m]/25g ball)

# fire

SUNKISSED
(page 76)

Young Touch Cotton DK by
Estelle Designs (100%
mercerized cotton; 114yds
[105m]/50g ball)

HEARTH
(page 80)
Cascade 220 by Cascade Yarns
(100% wool; 220yds
[201m]/100g skein)

GLOWING
(page 84)
18/24 Wool by Mission Falls
(100% wool; 85yds
[78m]/50g ball)

KINDLE
(page 88)
Sport Weight Alpaca by Blue
Sky Alpacas (100% alpaca;
110yds [100m]/50g skein)

TOASTY
(page 94)
Falk by Dale of Norway (100%
wool; 116yds [106m]/50g ball)

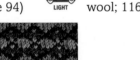

# earth

PEAT
(page 102)
Tussock by Naturally (85% wool,
15% polyester; 203yds
[185m]/100g ball)

Naturelle DK by Naturally
(100% wool; 210yds
[192m]/100g ball)

GLEN
(page 108)
Classic Wool by Patons (100%
wool; 223yds [204m]/100g ball)

PETROGLYPH
(page 114)
Hempwol by Lanaknits Designs
(50% hemp, 50% wool; 254yds
[240m]/100g skein)

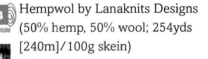

CANYON
(page 120)
Classic Wool by Patons (100%
wool; 223yds [204m]/100g ball)

TUNDRA
(page 126)
Morehouse Merino 2-Ply by
Morehouse Farm (100% wool;
220yds [201m]/50g skein)

Suggested substitutions:
For Young Touch Cotton DK by Estelle Designs-Isis by Scheepjes,
   available from JCA, Inc.
For Merino/Alpaca by SweaterKits-Ultra Alpaca by Berroco, Inc.

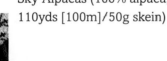

# yarn suppliers

The materials used in this book are available at fine local yarn and craft stores everywhere. We've provided this listing of retailers and wholesalers to assist you in finding the closest supplier, or, where noted, to assist in finding an item that is a little more difficult to get.

**Berroco, Inc.**
www.berroco.com
1-800-343-4948
PO Box 367
14 Elmdale Road
Uxbridge, MA 01569

**Blue Sky Alpacas, Inc.**
www.blueskyalpacas.com
1-888-460-8862
PO Box 88
Cedar, MN 55011

**Cascade Yarns**
www.cascadeyarns.com
1-800-548-1048
1224 Andover Park East
Tukwila, WA 98188

**Classic Elite Yarns**
www.classiceliteyarns.com
1-800-343-0308
122 Western Avenue
Lowell, MA 01851

**CNS Yarns**
1-877-244-1204
5333 Casgrain Avenue, Suite 1204
Montreal, QC H2T 1X3
Canada

**Dale of Norway, Inc.**
www.dale.no
1-800-441-3253
4750 Shelburne Road, Suite 2
Shelburne, VT 05482
in Canada available from Estelle Designs

Diamond Yarn
www.diamondyarn.com
1-800-268-1896
9697 St. Laurent, Suite 101
Montreal, QC H3L 2N1
Canada
or
115 Martin Ross, Unit #3
Toronto, ON M3J 2L9
Canada

Estelle Designs and Sales, Ltd.
www.estelledesigns.ca
1-800-387-5167
2220 Midland Aveue, Units 65/67
Scarborough, ON M1P 3E6
Canada

Fiber Trends
www.fibertrends.com
1-888-733-5991
315 Colorado Park Place
East Wenatchee, WA 98802

JCA, Inc.
www.jcacrafts.com
1-800-225-6340
35 Scales Lane
Townsend, MA 01469

King Cole Yarns
Available from Cascade Yarns
in Canada available from Estelle Designs.

Lanaknits Designs
www.hempforknitting.com
1-888-301-0011
320 Vernon Street, Suite 3B
Nelson, BC V1L 4E4
Canada

Lana Grossa
www.lanagrossa.com
Available from Unicorn Books and Crafts, Inc.,
in Canada available from Estelle Designs.

Mission Falls
www.missionfalls.com
Available from CNS Yarns.

Morehouse Farm
www.morehousefarm.com
1-866-470-4852
141 Milan Hill Road
Milan, NY 12571

Naturally Yarns
Available from Fiber Trends
in Canada available from The Old Mill
Knitting Company.

Needful Yarns
www.needfulyarnsinc.com
1-866-800-4700
60 Industrial Parkway, PMB #233
Cheektowaga, NY 14227
or
4476 Chesswood Drive, Unit 10-11
Toronto, ON M3J 2B9
Canada

Patons
www.patonsyarns.com
1-888-368-8401
320 Livingston Aveue South
Listowel, ON N4W 3H3
Canada

Sweaterkits
www.sweaterkits.com
1-877-232-9415
PO Box 397
Sharon, ON L0G 1VO
Canada

The Old Mill Knitting Company
www.oldmillknitting.com
866-964-9941
PO Box 81176
Ancaster, ON L9G 4X2
Canada

Unicorn Books and Crafts, Inc.
www.unicornbooks.com
1-800-289-9276
1388 Ross Street
Petaluma, CA 94954

# acknowledgments

Strangely enough, this is the most difficult part of the book to write. This is the point where I discovered that my command of the English language is not deep enough to convey the level of gratitude that I feel toward the team of people who surrounded me while I worked on this project. Their expertise, hard work, and willingness to go the extra mile to give me just what I needed amazed me. Many of these people have been part of my team for a long time now, and the fact that they continue to work unfailingly and with great humor, sometimes under duress . . . well, words fail me.

My test knitters, technical editor, and graphic designer put in many long hours and gave freely of their knowledge and skill: Joan Kass, Wannietta Prescod, Carole Herbert, Carol Corsetti, Sandra Whittaker, Susan Preston, Susan Kulczycki, Gayle Bunn, and Rebecca Cober. Thanks to the models for their time and smiles: Rebecca, Liz, Ryan, Fiona, Charlotte, Jennilu, and Jessica. Thanks again to Lindsey Maier for the wonderful photography. I truly value the support of my agent Linda Roghaar and editor Mona Michael, also Rosy Ngo and all the team at Potter Craft. Without the support of the yarn companies, sourcing the yarns for the garments would be so much harder, so thank you for all your advice and speedy responses.

I have an incredible circle of friends and family who extend their support to me even when I am being antisocial, burying myself in pattern instructions and yarn. So I thank you all for your patience and for being my cheerleaders, particularly to Paula, who, even though she hates to fly, will get on a plane to come to wish me well on my special occasions. Also a special thanks to Rebecca, who is always there with help, advice, and a smile, and doesn't think that I am strange for carrying my hard drive around in my purse when the deadline for the manuscript is looming. My most special thanks go to Rob, who continues to show himself as my number one fan: I don't deserve you, but thanks for all that you do for me!

# suggested further reading

Investigate these wonderful books to learn more about the "elemental" stories that helped inspire the garments in this book. I hope they'll inspire you, too.

*The Natural Year*, by Jane Alexander (Avon Books, 1997)

*The Book of the Year: A Brief History of Our Seasonal Holidays*, by Anthony Aveni (Oxford University Press, 2003)

*Bright Earth: Art and the Invention of Color*, by Philip Ball (Farrar, Straus & Giroux, 2001)

*The Hungry Woman: Myths and Legends of the Aztecs*, edited by John Bierhorst (William Morrow and Co, Inc., 1984)

*Festivals of the World*, by Elizabeth Breuilly, Joanne O'Brien, and Martin Palmer (Checkmark Books, 2002)

*Color: A Course in Mastering the Art of Mixing Colors*, by Betty Edwards (Tarcher, 2004)

*Colour*, by Edith Anderson Feisner (Laurence King Publishing, 2001)

*Colour: Travels through the Paintbox*, Victoria Finlay (Hodder and Stoughton, 2002)

*The Secret Language of Symbols*, by David Fontana (Chronicle Books, 1993)

*Mauve*, by Simon Garfield (Faber and Faber, 2000)

*Folklore of World Holidays*, by Robert Griffin and Ann Shurgin (Gale Research 1999)

*Earth, Air, Fire, and Water*, Juliet Heslewood (Oxford University Press, 1985)

*Hokusai*, by J. Hillier (Phaidon Press, 1978)

*Myths of the Ancient Greeks*, by Richard Martin (Penguin Books, 2003)

*The Timeline Book of the Arts*, by George Ochoa and Melinda Corey (Random House, 1995)

*Festive India*, by Arun Sanon (Frank Brothers & Co., 1987)

*Holiday Symbols and Customs*, by Sue Ellen Thompson (Omnigraphics, 2003)

*The Mystery of the Periodic Table*, by Benjamin Wiker (Ignatius Press, 2003)

# websites

For more information on well dressing (page 29), Tibetan prayer flags (page 65), Greek mythology (page 69), Aztec creation stories (page 83), and glassmaking (page 87), visit the following sites:

www.cressbrook.co.uk

www.derbyshire-peakdistrict.co.uk

www.khandro.net

www.welldressing.com

# index